NEW DIRECTIONS FOR TEACHING AND LEARNING

Robert J. Menges, *Northwestern University*
EDITOR-IN-CHIEF

Marilla D. Svinicki, *University of Texas, Austin*
ASSOCIATE EDITOR

Teaching and Learning at a Distance: What It Takes to Effectively Design, Deliver, and Evaluate Programs

Thomas E. Cyrs
New Mexico State University

EDITOR

Number 71, Fall 1997

JOSSEY-BASS PUBLISHERS
San Francisco

TEACHING AND LEARNING AT A DISTANCE: WHAT IT TAKES
TO EFFECTIVELY DESIGN, DELIVER, AND EVALUATE PROGRAMS
Thomas E. Cyrs (ed.)
New Directions for Teaching and Learning, no. 71
Robert J. Menges, Editor-in-Chief
Marilla D. Svinicki, Associate Editor

Microfilm copies of issues and articles are available in 16mm and 35mm, as well as microfiche in 105mm, through University Microfilms Inc., 300 North Zeeb Road, Ann Arbor, Michigan 48106-1346.

ISSN 0271-0633   ISBN 0-7879-9884-2

NEW DIRECTIONS FOR TEACHING AND LEARNING is part of The Jossey-Bass Higher and Adult Education Series and is published quarterly by Jossey-Bass Inc., Publishers, 350 Sansome Street, San Francisco, California 94104-1342. Periodicals postage paid at San Francisco, California, and at additional mailing offices. POSTMASTER: Send address changes to New Directions for Teaching and Learning, Jossey-Bass Inc., Publishers, 350 Sansome Street, San Francisco, California 94104-1342.

New Directions for Teaching and Learning is indexed in College Student Personnel Abstracts, Contents Pages in Education, and Current Index to Journals in Education (ERIC).

SUBSCRIPTIONS cost $54.00 for individuals and $90.00 for institutions, agencies, and libraries. Prices subject to change.

EDITORIAL CORRESPONDENCE should be sent to the editor-in-chief, Robert J. Menges, Northwestern University, Center for the Teaching Professions, 2115 North Campus Drive, Evanston, Illinois 60208-2610.

Cover photograph by Richard Blair/Color & Light © 1990.

Jossey-Bass Web address: http://www.josseybass.com

Printed in the United States of America on acid-free recycled paper containing 100 percent recovered waste paper, of which at least 20 percent is postconsumer waste.

CONTENTS

98196

FROM THE SERIES EDITORS

About This Publication. Since 1980, *New Directions for Teaching and Learning* (NDTL) has brought a unique blend of theory, research, and practice to leaders in postsecondary education. NDTL sourcebooks strive not only for solid substance but also for timeliness, compactness, and accessibility.

The series has four goals: to inform readers about current and future directions in teaching and learning in postsecondary education, to illuminate the context that shapes these new directions, to illustrate these new directions through examples from real settings, and to propose ways in which these new directions can be incorporated into still other settings.

This publication reflects our view that teaching deserves respect as a high form of scholarship. We believe that significant scholarship is conducted not only by researchers who report results of empirical investigations but also by practitioners who share disciplined reflections about teaching. Contributors to NDTL approach questions of teaching and learning as seriously as they approach substantive questions in their own disciplines, and they deal not only with pedagogical issues but also with the intellectual and social context in which these issues arise. Authors deal on the one hand with theory and research and on the other with practice, and they translate from research and theory to practice and back again.

About This Volume. In this volume, a group of experienced distance educators describe how this new form of teaching and learning differs from the standard classroom and how teachers and learners will both need to develop new skills and new ways of thinking. In light of the explosion of multimedia-based instruction and the possibilities it offers for new forms of instruction, their insights provide a look into the next area of faculty development.

Robert J. Menges, *Editor-in-Chief*
Marilla D. Svinicki, *Associate Editor*

EDITOR'S NOTES

Teaching at a distance is different from traditional teaching. Many of the skills of good teaching transfer to a distance learning environment, but some additional teaching skills are required. Any instructor who has taught through telephone conferencing, interactive television, on the Internet or World Wide Web, or through desktop television will confirm this assertion. Too many instructors have been informed that there are no differences or only "minor" adjustments to be made for distance teaching. They have been told that they can transport existing lecture-based courses to interactive television or telephone or other technologies without any modification or conversion. The result has been teaching by appendage, particularly on instructional television. This is characterized by untrained instructors' "moving hands," "hairy arms," or "shiny rings" as they teach with the technology ("'Virtual' Campuses . . . ," 1996).

Many academic administrators act as though distance learning was their field of dreams. Build the teleclassrooms, purchase the latest technology, and the students will come. Often forgotten is the training that the instructors needed for quality distance learning programs. Thornburg (1992, p. 49) notes that "technology, by itself, is neutral. . . . It is essential that we place pedagogy above technology." Students do not learn from the technology. They learn from competent instructors who have been trained how to communicate through the technology. Knowing what the strengths and weaknesses of the delivery systems are, they can capitalize on the advantages and minimize or circumvent the restrictions.

As distance learning (or distributive learning, as it will be called in the future) proliferates at a dizzying pace in all areas of education and training, the need for instructor training in teaching at a distance will become obvious. Student consumers will begin to discriminate among those courses that have simply been transported without modification and those courses that have been modified or specifically designed for teaching at a distance. It is incumbent on postsecondary administrators as well as corporate, government, and other user groups to provide the needed support and training for instructors who will be required to teach through any delivery technology, whether it be interactive video, telephone, desktop video, or the World Wide Web.

The conceptual outline for this issue of *New Directions for Teaching and Learning* is concerned with teaching and learning in a distance learning environment, rather than administrative and policy issues only. Each author was requested to walk into an imaginary distance classroom and view everything from the point of view of the instructor and student. They were asked how instruction and learning could best be supported. This issue is broken down into four parts: "Issues and Trends," "Instructional Design Principles for Distance Learning," "Alternative Delivery Systems for Distance Learning," and "Administrative Issues for the Distance Instructor." Each author presents the state of the art in his or her field. Note the repeated call for staff development and the need for visualization, interactivity, and team support.

Part One, Issues and Trends, begins the issue with a discussion by George P. Connick, in Chapter One, of the changes in higher education that were sown immediately after World War II and that have been growing slowly until today. Because the variables in higher education are shifting, he challenges us to think beyond the traditional to a vision of the university that moves past the barriers of time and place to knowledge available to all at any time in any place from multiple institutions. This will require policy changes in four areas: universal access, quality of programs based on learning outcomes, student service centers able to respond quickly to student needs, and productivity—doing more for less.

Part Two, Instructional Design Principles for Distance Learning, deals with several key areas: instructor skills, interactivity, visual thinking, and learning principles for the design of telecourses and beyond. It begins in Chapter Two with an outline by Thomas E. Cyrs of the kinds of skills instructors need to develop to teach effectively with technology. These skills differ significantly from those used in the standard classroom setting.

In Chapter Three, Ellen D. Wagner distinguishes between interaction and interactivity. The former takes place between two or more students, and the latter refers to the ability to make connections with people through the technology. She notes that the importance of interactions during instruction is to move the student toward goal achievement.

The importance of visual thinking for visual technologies is stressed by Cyrs in Chapter Four. Three types of visual symbols used in visual thinking are reviewed, and the concept of "word pictures" is stressed. The latter consists of geometric shapes with key words and phrases connected by markers that show the visual-spatial relationships among ideas as one communicates. Word pictures can help students determine the importance and interrelationships of ideas.

A review of the research about the learner variables and teaching strategies that need to be considered in achieving positive outcomes for telecourse students is presented in Chapter Five. M. Winston Egan and Gordon S. Gibb provide evidence for the effectiveness of such things as developing learning communities electronically, using active learning to promote student engagement at field sites, and using feedback to promote learning.

Student development before and during a telecourse has been a neglected topic in many distance learning programs. Darcy Walsh Hardy and Mary H. Boaz, in Chapter Six, focus attention on the need to prepare students to be successful in a telecourse beyond mastering the technology. They share the results of their study of student needs, which indicates that these students have need for the same data as on-campus students. The authors recommend that a student handbook specific to distance learning be provided to students.

Part Three, Alternative Delivery Systems for Distance Learning, explores some of the alternatives available to the teleinstructor and the positives and negatives of each. In Chapter Seven, Virginia A. Ostendorf stresses the need to focus on the learner rather than the instructor in live video instruction. She emphasizes three components: learner-centered design, learner-centered delivery skills, and learner participation.

The oldest delivery system is POTS, plain old telephone service, described in Chapter Eight. In use at the University of Wisconsin since the 1960s, it still offers many inexpensive advantages. Christine H. Olgren reviews the strengths and weaknesses of this delivery system. Coupled with well-designed student study guides, the telephone is an effective, efficient, and relatively inexpensive delivery system.

An outline of the basic features of the Internet and World Wide Web environment is presented in Chapter Nine by Rory McGreal. In addition to presenting important suggestions on course design, the chapter concludes with questions that an instructor should consider before engaging in Web-based courses.

In Chapter Ten, Alan G. Chute, Pamela K. Sayers, and Richard P. Gardner demonstrate that the center of networked learning environments is in desktop video teleconferencing and interactive group video teleconferencing. This technology merges voice, television, computing, and print in both real-time and delayed-time interactions. It is one of the most advanced conceptualizations currently in use and brings together all of the other technologies and instructional design principles.

Part Four, Administrative Issues for the Distance Instructor, alerts the reader to some important support considerations in distance education. For example, in Chapter Eleven, Michael R. Simonson recommends the use of eclectic models of evaluation for telecourses that use both quantitative and qualitative approaches. He provides the reader with ideas about areas to explore when developing an evaluation plan for distance learning.

What we design into telecourses for any system will be strongly affected by current copyright law. Instructors must be knowledgeable about what they can and cannot use because these courses could be highly visible beyond the traditional campus. In Chapter Twelve, Janis H. Bruwelheide brings the reader up to date on these issues. "Fair use" for distance educators is reviewed, and some important specific suggestions for distance instructors are provided.

In the years ahead the traditional library will make the transition to an information center where the functions of the librarians and the services they offer will change dramatically. In Chapter Thirteen, Roberta L. Derlin and Edward Erazo explore this impending change.

Finally, in Chapter Fourteen, Richard S. Tolsma identifies one of the greatest challenges faced by institutions that have or are developing distance learning programs: to create integrated, easily accessed, high-quality student information services. He poses six questions that, if answered, will go a long way toward determining the features of the information and service systems that must be established.

In summary, these chapters are practical and utilitarian. They address many questions about teaching at a distance in a variety of different delivery systems. Individually and collectively, they will serve as a solid foundation for instructor training and administrative policy making in a distance learning environment.

References

Thornburg, D. D. *Edutrends 2010: Restructuring, Technology, and the Future of Education.* San Carlos, Calif.: Starsong Publications, 1992.
"'Virtual' Campuses Are Decades Away—At Least." *Boston Globe,* July 14, 1996, p. 44:1.

THOMAS E. CYRS is professor of educational management and development in the College of Education and the senior faculty adviser for teaching in the Center for Educational Development at New Mexico State University. He is also president of Educational Development Associates.

Part One

Issues and Trends

Higher education at the beginning of the next century will be structured very differently than it is today. This chapter explores how technological change will influence the evolution of new institutional structures.

Issues and Trends to Take Us into the Twenty-First Century

George P. Connick

What will higher education look like in the first decade of the twenty-first century? While there are a wide variety of answers to this question, some things are reasonably clear. The future will be forged from the capacities we have today and those that we develop tomorrow. Most importantly, the future will be shaped by the educational vision of our leaders.

If ten people were asked to describe their first image when they hear the word *university*, most would respond with similar descriptions—a campus, large buildings, teachers and students in classrooms or laboratories, students living in dormitories, sports, and so on. If then asked what higher education might look like in 2005, most would probably respond with a similar description. It is very difficult for most people, including those in academe, to conceive of any significant change in the higher education structure that is in place today.

In fact, the seeds of change for twenty-first-century education were sown in the years after World War II and have been germinating slowly for fifty years. The first blooms of the diverse educational landscape of the future are just beginning to be seen.

The Reality of Change

The roots of cultural change, and its scope, are often difficult to understand when one is in the midst of the maelstrom. And change is often unwelcome; we are most comfortable with the known and familiar.

There is a wonderful, three-hour program that was first shown on public broadcasting stations in June 1996, entitled *Triumph of the Nerds* (Segaler,

1996). The program aptly illustrates this resistance to change and offers a striking parallel to the situation in higher education today.

Triumph of the Nerds chronicles the history of the great innovations in computers and telecommunications through the words and actions of the pioneers and innovators. We hear from Wozniak, Jobs, Gates, and a slew of others.

A portion of this program also addresses Xerox's research activities in the 1970s and 1980s at the Palo Alto Research Center—PARC for short. This latter segment was chronicled in depth in a wonderful book written in 1988 by Douglas K. Smith and Robert C. Alexander titled *Fumbling the Future: How XEROX Invented, then Ignored, the First Personal Computer* (Smith and Alexander, 1988). In 1973, many years before Apple or IBM released their first personal computers, scientists at Xerox's PARC produced the Alto, the first computer designed for individual use. By 1976, PARC's researchers had completed a system of personal computing hardware and software not matched in the marketplace for nearly ten years, until the Macintosh computer was introduced. Remarkably, these groundbreaking inventions were never exploited by Xerox.

What happened? Why didn't Xerox forge to the lead in this emerging industry? According to the authors, "Their actions reflected all the complexities of Xerox's corporate culture of the mid-1970s: a one product monopoly facing competition for the first time and losing market share, an organization grown bloated and complacent after more than a decade of unprecedented prosperity, a numbers-oriented, nontechnical, and risk-averse top management committed to the notion that, to be safe, change required a protracted period of testing and review" (p. 8).

The Xerox PARC story of twenty years ago mirrors the situation facing higher education today. Higher education's current structure was created during the lifetime of people born since 1945. The great expansion of public higher education took place after World War II with the return of the veterans, the launching of the G.I. Bill, and the great baby boom of the late 1940s and 1950s. Across America, hundreds of new institutions were created and hundreds of others expanded. And the planners used the only model of higher education they knew—one that was labor-intensive and campus based. In 1950, approximately 90 percent of the students attending college were between the ages of eighteen and twenty-one. Most were not only young but full-time students. A large percentage lived in campus residence halls. Campuses as small cities, with a plethora of services for students, made sense through the 1960s and 1970s.

But in the 1970s change was under way in American society. A service and information economy began to replace the industrial economy. Of significance for education, the number of eighteen-year-olds began to decline. To bolster enrollments, colleges began to recruit adults.

Today the educational landscape is strikingly different. Only 52 percent of college students are eighteen to twenty-one, and fewer than 15 percent fit the profile of the residential student—young, full-time, and living on campus.

As a result of changing economic and social conditions in the United States and around the world, America approaches the twenty-first century with more than thirty-six hundred accredited institutions that were built in a different era, for a different student population, with a very different set of economic realities. Our educational institutions reflect their industrial-era roots. They are organized around centralized structures (similar to the factory model) by aggregating the workers (faculty and students) at a particular place (the campus) at a particular time (the academic calendar).

Just as the American economy has moved away from the industrial model to one that is information based, technology intensive, niche oriented, and decentralized, so will education have to change. At the beginning of the twenty-first century, higher education will be in the middle of a major transformation. Access to education will be available to the population at large from a number of providers via information technology and telecommunications. It is likely to be available anywhere and anytime that the consumer wants it. Most importantly, consumers will have the choice of enrolling in courses and earning degrees from multiple institutions without ever leaving their homes. Moreover, there will be options for converting one's knowledge, however acquired (for example, through self-instruction, military training, corporate seminars, and so on), into certified competencies. At this point, the control of education will have shifted from the provider to the consumer.

Education as a public monopoly will cease to exist. The future for most institutions will be determined by the extent to which they have an educational product or products that are provided conveniently for the consumer at a competitive cost.

Our educational culture—a culture based on the campus, the classroom, and on teaching in a time-specific way—has been in place for several hundred years. For the first time in its history, new demographic realities and a formidable new culture are challenging the very foundation of the traditional culture. The new culture is based on the power and the dynamic nature of information technology and telecommunications, which, combined, allow us to deliver education anywhere, at any time, to anyone who needs it. In other words, the historical raison d'être for campuses—the need to aggregate human and physical resources at a single location at a specific time in order to serve the large number of students who could come to that location—has a major competitor.

For the first time, educational consumers have choices regarding what, when, where, how, and from whom they can secure an education. Those choices will expand at an exponential rate as we move into the next century. Location will offer little competitive advantage to most institutions. Potential students will shop for institutions that provide the most efficient and most student-centered services, whenever the student needs them, with the highest quality and the lowest cost.

Understandably, the reality of an educational structure freed from the constraints of place and time is both difficult to understand for some and enormously threatening to others. For at least a decade, most campuses have treated the new technologies as something they must contend with—computer labs, for example—but they have tended to regard technology as a fringe function of the real work of the academy. But rather than remaining on the fringe, the wedding of distance education, information technology, and telecommunications into a powerful new educational structure has served as the catalyst for an educational paradigm shift that is well under way.

Distance education is one of the most powerful new forces influencing the direction of education. It is already well established in many countries around the world. The challenge for the educational community in the United States in the next few years is to bring information technology and telecommunications to the core of higher education. To do this requires that we actually use these powerful new technologies to restructure education to serve learners better and more cost-effectively. Otherwise, change imposed from outside the academy will force us to achieve public policy goals.

Richard D. Lamm, former governor of Colorado, quotes Joseph Schumpeter, Nobel Prize–winning economist, who observed that "all human institutions eventually become smug, self-satisfied, incestuous, bureaucratic, inefficient and risk-adverse. Time and past success cause them to lose the cutting edge vitality that made them great institutions in the first place" (Lamm, 1996, p. 23).

It was to some extent the frustration public policy makers felt with the higher education establishment that led to an event that is likely to be viewed in future years as a defining moment in the history of higher education. And it occurred just as higher education neared the end of the century in which it experienced its golden era. That powerful symbol of educational change was the creation on June 24, 1996, of the Western Governors' University (WGU). This new institution was launched when 10 western governors adopted the implementation plan for a totally new type of institution. The WGU will be a fully accredited, degree-granting institution that draws on the curriculum and faculty resources of numerous institutions (public and private, educational and corporate) to provide learners with broad access to education at a distance. Moreover, a range of student services will be provided through electronic and other nontraditional means. But probably of most significance to both students and traditional institutions is the shift from "inputs" to "outcomes." The WGU will not be focused on the number of traditional credit courses a student accumulates but rather on certifying the learning outcomes that he or she has achieved. Thus, a student may demonstrate competency in a variety of ways, such as through self-instruction and military training, in addition to traditional credit courses.

The Scope of Change

Nicholas Negroponte, the head of the Media Lab at MIT, says that "bits (0s and 1s), which are the DNA of information," are rapidly replacing atoms as the "basic commodity of human interaction. Computers, in the next few years, will be freed from the confines of keyboards and screens—they will become objects that we talk to, drive with, touch or even wear" (Negroponte, 1995, p. 6).

Expressed somewhat differently, the digital age will allow us to move images of every sort far more efficiently and cost-effectively than we can move people. We will be able to connect students and others to the educational experience they need, in real time or asynchronously, regardless of whether it is by voice, video, or data. Technically, the barriers to change are falling rapidly, and by the beginning of the next century we will have unparalleled technological capacity to link learners with educational providers.

In their perceptive book entitled *Paradigm Shift: The New Promise of Information Technology,* Don Tapscott and Art Caston (1993) offer some hope that change can be accommodated. They state that "old paradigms die hard. Whether they regard the flat world, Newtonian physics, or the first era of information technology, old paradigms and their corresponding attitudes, institutions, and cultures have built-in resistance to their own self-destruction. But they also contain the seeds of their own creative transformation. An outmoded paradigm in its death agony calls forth leaders for the new" (p. 281).

The most critical issue affecting the role of higher education in the next decade is not technological. The real issue is leadership. Will higher education be able to shift from an industrial model to an information age model? Who will lead the way?

Recognizing that embedded cultures have great difficulty changing but that dynamic new forces will make change inevitable, we can expect a period of controversy and conflict in higher education. And, in fact, this is occurring as the forces of resistance to change are mobilizing to protect the status quo.

Regardless of the turmoil that may ensue, it is likely that change will occur in four major educational policy areas.

Access. We might reasonably assume that access to educational opportunity will become universal. The real challenge for the future will be redefining access to mean universal access for both faculty and students to the information technology that will make higher education meaningful. Broadly defined, information technology will include not only ownership (possession) of the necessary hardware and software but also training on demand in its use and application as well as help desk support.

Quality. There will be a shift from measuring educational inputs (for example, the number of faculty with Ph.D.'s) to measuring educational outcomes. There will be less emphasis on evaluating how well a faculty member has taught and more on what students have learned. In addition, the academic enterprise will begin to move along a continuum from almost totally synchronous instruction to instruction that is much more asynchronous. Again, this will place more learning options in the hands of consumers.

Efficiency. To support the academic enterprise and a changing student population, the administrative and student service functions will experience significant transformation. Technology will stimulate multicampus (public or private) consolidation of many of the nonacademic functions (such as registration, financial aid, and so on) of institutions into "service centers" that are able to respond quickly and efficiently to student needs. Staffed by highly trained, student-oriented professionals, many of these centers are likely to be outsourced to organizations that specialize in these functions for multiple campuses, probably spanning large geographic areas including multiple states.

Productivity. Doing more with less will be the major agenda of higher education in the immediate future. The labor- and facilities-intensive current structure will be reassessed, and the result will be reorganization and downsizing in order to survive tight budgetary times and the competition from institutions that are more technologically agile.

Conclusion

The approval of the Western Governors' University in a remarkably short span of time indicates the speed with which a new educational culture is emerging. This issue of *New Directions for Teaching and Learning* documents the details of a transformation that is already well under way. These changes are not aberrations or fads. The origins are found in the development of the British Open University, the Open Learning Agency of British Columbia, the National Technological University, the University of Phoenix, the Education Network of Maine, and many others.

The question is not whether a new higher education paradigm will develop but rather how fast it will occur. Although we cannot yet fully answer the question asked at the beginning of this chapter, we can begin to see an outline of higher education that is easier to access, unconstrained by barriers of space and time, student centered, and cost-effective. For now, that appears to be a sufficient answer.

References

Lamm, R. D. "Futurizing America's Institutions." *The Futurist,* 1996, *30,* pp. 23–26.
Negroponte, N. *Being Digital.* New York: Knopf, 1995.
Segaler, S. (producer). *Triumph of the Nerds.* Portland: Oregon Public Broadcasting, 1996.
Smith, D. K., and Alexander, R. C. *Fumbling the Future: How XEROX Invented, then Ignored, the First Personal Computer.* New York: Morrow, 1988.
Tapscott, D., and Caston, A. *Paradigm Shift: The New Promise of Information Technology.* New York: McGraw-Hill, 1993.

GEORGE P. CONNICK *is president of Distance Education Publictions, Inc., and president emeritus of the Education Network of Maine.*

Part Two

Instructional Design Principles for Distance Learning

Instructors need special skills and sensitivities to be competent in distance education.

Competence in Teaching at a Distance

Thomas E. Cyrs

"Just go in there and teach the way you have always taught. There isn't any difference between traditional classroom teaching and teaching at a distance." This often-repeated statement by poorly informed administrators perpetuates the myth that no additional training is necessary to go from the classroom to the studio. This is exactly what some administrators want to hear. They reason that if there are only minor differences, then instructors don't need additional training, and this keeps the budgets down. This reasoning leads to telecourses that simply shift the same pedagogy currently prominent in traditional college classrooms, the passive lecture, to teleclassrooms. The "talking head" predominates.

Institutions that perpetuate this attitude and do not provide training for distance learning instructors will not survive in the growing student consumer market. Those telecourses that have been designed or modified for mediated communication in real and delayed time and whose instructors have been trained to take advantage of the visual and interactive nature of the growing variety of delivery systems will be the choice of potential students.

The purpose of this chapter is to lay out some of the skills and strategies that will help instructors make a difference in teaching at a distance. Instructors who are able to put these ideas into practice will be designing courses that will both appeal to and teach the distance students more effectively.

Competencies for Distance Teaching

There are a number of areas of competence that relate to teaching at a distance, especially on interactive television, both live and taped. These competencies have been reported in four separate studies that used surveys and interviews with a variety of populations and situations. Three studies (Cyrs and Smith,

1988, 1990; Thach, 1994) have dealt with distance learning in academic institutions, and one (Chute, Balthazan, and Posten, 1988) has dealt with training in a corporate setting. All four studies identified many of the same general areas of competence, with a few exceptions. These general areas of competence in the individual studies are grouped below with the study or studies citing that area as important.

The areas of competence identified by all four studies (Cyrs and Smith, 1988, 1990; Chute, Balthazan, and Posten, 1988; Thach, 1994) are discussed below.

Course planning and organization. This area includes a knowledge of how teleteaching differs from traditional teaching and how the capabilities, advantages, and disadvantages of the delivery system affect the course plan. It also includes logistical knowledge such as copyright issues, the use of site coordinators, and technical details such as moving instructional materials (tests, homework, handouts, and so on) back and forth between sites. This area encompasses more basic course design strategies such as how to build interactive teaching/learning strategies into the course, how to use technologies effectively, and general knowledge of instructional development and systems theory. It also includes knowledge about learning theory and how it can be used to design more effective teaching for distance learning.

Verbal and nonverbal presentation skills. It is important for all teachers to be able to construct an organized presentation, to project enthusiasm for the topic, and to be able to pace a lecture appropriately. However, in addition, the teleinstructor must be able to coordinate any presentation with the study guide or handout being used by the off-site learners. This type of presentation uses keywords and phrases as fill-ins to cue students, focus their attention, and keep everyone together. An added difficulty for the distance instructor is that he or she is operating under a severe reduction in feedback cues from the learners about pacing and understanding. Additionally, the teleinstructor must be aware of how he or she looks, sounds, and moves on television. Some instructor characteristics are exaggerated, while others are diminished by the medium. Finally, because there is a premium on student interaction, the teleinstructor needs to know how to manage discussion among field sites as well as with the students at the origination site.

Collaborative teamwork. It will be noted in later chapters that distance teaching is more of a team effort than classroom instruction is. It is also the case that distance students need to depend on one another for a lot of their learning. Therefore, the teleinstructor needs to know how to work as part of a team and to help students work as parts of teams as well.

Questioning strategies. As noted above, interaction is an important part of distance teaching. Teleteachers need to know how to construct questions at a variety of intellectual levels and for a variety of instructional purposes and to move among these levels and purposes during a questioning interlude. He or she should know how to establish ground rules for asking and answering questions and how to signal which individuals and sites should respond. He or she should also know how to encourage students to ask questions and how to provide positive feedback verbally and nonverbally when they do.

Subject matter expertise. While it almost goes without saying that the teleinstructor needs to have a solid mastery of the subject matter, he or she should also understand how that subject matter will be learned by the students and what examples, analogies, visuals, and other supports will support that learning.

Involving students and coordinating their activities at field sites. This may be one of the key differences between teleteaching and classroom instruction because in addition to keeping students involved, the teleinstructor is doing it while trying to coordinate the activities of several remote sites. This means designing courses that maximize student involvement at the field sites from 30 percent to 50 percent of class time and managing students in timed activities and exercises without actually being present. To do this the instructor will need to understand how to select, design, or adapt exercises to match the domain, intellectual skill level, and cognitive level of the course objectives, while still making them clear enough to allow students at remote sites to engage in them without much direct supervision.

The following additional areas were identified by only one study.

Basic learning theory (Chute, Balthazan, and Posten, 1988). Knowledge of a variety of learning theories will help instructors adapt to differences in learners as well as to differences in context.

Knowledge of the distance learning field (Thach, 1994). This might be considered a given. However, lack of knowledge of the variety of delivery systems and their ability to provide synchronous and asynchronous communications will limit the breadth of teaching possibilities.

Design of study guides correlated with the television screen (Cyrs and Smith, 1988, 1990). Study guides enhance the instructor's delivery and provide an outline of the presentation by limiting the amount of note-copying and providing a conceptual outline for the student. Several study guide formats exist that can be used as learning management tools before, during, and after a teleclass. All parts of the study guide are correlated with pictures and graphics that appear on the television screen or with a presentation using either audio or computer conferencing.

Graphic design and visual thinking (Cyrs and Smith, 1988, 1990). Television is a visual medium in any format, and instructors need to be taught to visualize their ideas. Instructors should be able to communicate ideas as pictures, graphics, and artifacts, alone and complemented by key words and phrases. Visual thinking can also be represented with word pictures. Instructors may also need to redesign graphic and pictorial materials from any source, including textbooks, to meet the requirements of an aspect ratio appropriate to television or computer monitor. They should have a knowledge of basic graphic design principles for television and computing and an understanding of visual communication principles and techniques.

Conclusion

Anyone who says that teaching at a distance is the same as traditional teaching is dead wrong. Instructors need more planning time, more instructional support, and additional training to modify courses for all of the potential delivery formats for distance teaching. Institutions planning on making incursions into the distance education area should be considering the capabilities of the faculty along with the capabilities of the technology and providing for both.

References

Chute, A., Balthazan, L. B., and Posten, C. O. "Learning from Teletraining." *American Journal of Distance Education,* 1988, 2 (3), 55–63.

Cyrs, T., and Smith, F. A. "Faculty Training for Television Teaching: State of the Art." Paper presented at the Annual Conference of the Association for Educational Communications and Technology, New Orleans, 1988.

Cyrs, T., and Smith, F. A. *Teleclass Teaching: A Resource Guide.* (2nd ed.) Las Cruces: Center for Educational Development, New Mexico State University, 1990.

Thach, E. C. "Perceptions of Distance Education Experts Regarding the Roles, Outputs, and Competencies Needed in the Field of Distance Education." Unpublished doctoral dissertation, Texas A&M University, 1994.

THOMAS E. CYRS is professor of educational management and development in the College of Education and the senior faculty adviser for teaching in the Center for Educational Development at New Mexico State University. He is also president of Educational Development Associates.

Instructors are encouraged to build interactivity into distance learning,
but what does that mean exactly? This chapter promotes the concept
of interaction as a means to an end rather than an end in itself.

Interactivity: From Agents to Outcomes

Ellen D. Wagner

In the world of distance learning, very few topics have generated as much debate as the construct of interactivity. Distance learning practitioners—particularly instructors and program administrators—seem to view interactivity as the defining attribute of a contemporary distance learning experience. That is, the interactivity enabled by two-way technologies providing real-time exchanges of audio, video, text, and graphical information among distributed participants serves as one of distance learning's primary identifying characteristics.

The use of interactive technologies in a distance learning enterprise also contributes to perceptions of distance learning quality. For example, distance learning experiences that use interactive compressed video may be perceived as being "better" than a distance learning experience using workbooks and videotapes.

For critics, interactivity is frequently noted as the missing ingredient when comparing distance learning experiences with traditional face-to-face learning experiences. For proponents of distance learning, interactivity offers the evidence on which to build a case that a distance learning experience is just as good, if not better than, a traditional face-to-face learning experience.

Interactivity and the "New Media" of Distance Learning

If distance learning defines itself in large part by its dependence on interactive technologies, the increased capability for interactivity enabled by emerging technologies must also be factored into this discussion. High-performance computing and communications systems are resulting in the increased use of wireline technologies (such as desktop computers, compressed video, and laptop computers) to complement the conferencing technologies (for example, audioconferencing, videoconferencing, and computer-mediated conferencing) generally associated with distance learning. Wireless technologies (such as personal digital assistants, pagers, and cellular telephones, as well as remote/wireless network interfaces for PCS) make it possible to further extend interactive conferencing models. Finally, the emergence of the World Wide Web and its adaptation for deployment over the Internet and intranets provide a medium of information exchange whose significance as support tool is just now beginning to be realized.

Perhaps most exciting of all is the emergence of "new media" that enable the creation of new instructional experiences (Dede, 1997). These include

- Multimedia and hypermedia
- Computer-supported collaborative learning
- Interactive knowledge webs
- Virtual communities

Each of these new media represents a specific technology environment, providing unique opportunities for individual users to connect with information resources, instructional experiences, and other technologies *on terms established and defined by the users.* In these new technology-mediated learning environments, learners can function in self-directed ways while still receiving the support of the community with which they interact. By making learning location-independent, they push distance learning far beyond its current boundaries. Within this continually evolving context, it is increasingly important that the defining construct of interactivity be revisited.

Is It Interactivity—or Interaction?

In distance learning, interaction and interactivity are terms that are often used interchangeably, even thought there are several distinctions between them that are worth noting. Wagner (1994) defines interactions as reciprocal events requiring two objects and two actions. Interactions are suggested to occur when objects and events mutually influence one another. Interactivity, on the other hand, appears to emerge from descriptions of technological capability for establishing connections from point to point (or from point to multiple points) in real time. In Wagner's discussion, interactivity tends to focus on the attributes of the technology systems employed in distance learning enterprises. Conversely, interactions typically involve behaviors where individual and groups directly influence one another.

These distinctions are worth noting because they help to underscore the difficulty encountered when offering a description of this defining construct in operational, outcome-specific terms. Philosophical speculations on the role and effect of interaction are easier to generate than are working hypotheses that empirically determine the effect of interaction as a distance learning outcome.

Fascination with what technologies can do may actually confound a practitioner's emphasis on exploiting technologies to maximize teaching and learning outcomes in a distance learning context.

Interaction Agents

Attempting to bring a measure of order to discussions of interaction, Moore (1989) offers a schema in which he identifies three types of instructional interactions:

- Interactions that occur between the learner and the instructor
- Interactions that occur among learners
- Interactions that take place between learners and the content they are trying to master

One of the greatest benefits this has offered designers, implementers, and administrators of distance learning programs is a sense of direction to the transactions that are typically involved in a distance learning endeavor. Furthermore, Moore's interaction schema implies purpose, intent, and/or intended outcome of an interaction by virtue of indicating *who* or *what* is to be involved in a transaction. However, the explicit description of an interaction's purposes, intents, and outcomes are still left to the imagination. Moore's schema does not really describe the intended outcomes of these interaction categories. Instead it identifies the agents involved in or affected by a given interaction. In other words, it describes with whom—or with what—interactions will occur, within the context of a specific distance learning transaction.

Given the explosion of technology in the past decade, combined with the integration of interactive technologies in nearly every facet of life, it may be that focusing on real-time, technologically enabled interactivity as a defining attribute of distance learning is an artifact of the past. The value of interactive technologies as a resource for extending the reach of instruction and information can now more easily emerge as a means to an end. The earlier emphasis on the agents of an interaction can now help set the stage for a more meaningful discussion of the outcomes enabled by various types of interactions.

Interaction Outcomes

Focusing on the outcomes of interaction rather than the agents of interaction permits interactions to serve more effectively as a means to the end of performance improvement. In this context, interactions have two purposes: They must change learners, and they must move learners toward an action state of goal attainment.

By emphasizing the outcome of an interaction, one can see the effect that an interaction has on learners, whether the learner is in a distance learning endeavor or a traditional learning endeavor. Interactions enable active learner participation in the instructional/training/performance improvement process. They allow learners to tailor learning experiences to meet their specific needs or abilities. Interactions enable clarification and transfer of new ideas to already-held concept frameworks. Interactions promote intrinsic motivation on the part of a learner by highlighting the relevancy that new information may have under specific circumstances.

The significance of this shift in thinking can be more clearly recognized if we consider why a focus on outcomes of instruction is so important in this third decade of the "information age." Basic assumptions underlying the current systems available for educating children, for transitioning learning from school to the workplace, and for providing continuous learning opportunities in the workplace appear to be fundamentally flawed, given current social expectations of flexibility, adaptability, and creativity. Furthermore, in today's competitive global marketplace, organizational success regardless of level is increasingly built on a foundation of skilled, self-motivated, and engaged individuals with the capacity for managing their continuous learning needs. Basic literacy and numeric proficiency are necessary but no longer sufficient to be successful in school or in the workplace. Being able to think creatively, to solve problems, and to accommodate ambiguous situations are expected *in addition to* literacy and numeric skills. The evolving impact of technology on performance expectations adds to this mix. That is, if information is now assumed to be available at one's fingertips, it is far less critical that one memorize a massive store of facts and concepts when engaged in a learning endeavor. Instead, the ability to access, interpret, and apply information becomes a far more reasonable goal toward which to strive.

Types of Interactions

In building interaction into learning, the following types of interactions should be considered:

Interaction to increase participation. According to McCombs (1992), learning is a natural process of pursuing meaningful goals. It is active, volitional, and internally mediated, representing a process of discovering and constructing meaning from information and experience. Given this description, it is clear that learning depends in large part on an individual's willingness to engage in the learning process.

Interaction to increase participation. This type of interaction provides learners with a means of engagement. It may mean meeting fellow learners for the first time so that the basic level at which human relationships occur is established, or it may emphasize the willingness of individuals to assume leadership responsibilities for members of their particular cohort group.

Interaction to develop communication. Clearly articulating expectations, providing opportunities for personal expression, offering the ability to exchange information without fear of being judged or punished, persuading individuals to subscribe to a particular point of view or to recognize the value of making a change (whatever that change might be)—these are all examples of interactions for improving communications. Interaction offers the ability to share information and opinions or to intentionally influence the opinions or beliefs of others, all of which are germane to instructional, training, and/or performance support settings.

Interaction to receive feedback. Feedback refers to any information that allows learners to judge the quality of their performance. Wagner's (1994) review of feedback literature refers to a variety of conditions of feedback, noting that feedback tends to be considered from two differing perspectives. From a behavioristic perspective, feedback provides reinforcement, which is intended to correct and direct performance. Cognitivists suggest that feedback provides learners with information about the correctness of a response or allows learners to correct an incorrect response to enable long-term retention of correct information. In either case, learners need to obtain information from a variety of sources (from instructions, from other learners, from their own observations, from information resources) to judge the quality of their own performance.

Interaction to enhance elaboration and retention. From a cognitive perspective, elaborating on information (that is, coming up with alternative examples to explain a new idea, or developing alternative explanations for why an idea may be framed in a particular way) makes new information more meaningful for learners. By expanding or even manipulating a bit of information associated with a given idea, it is easier to recognize all of the various conceptual "hooks" that may be associated with that information. The extra cognitive "practice" that results from generating alternative interpretations make it easier for learners to integrate new information into their existing cognitive framework for enhanced long-term retention and recall.

Interaction to support learner control/self-regulation. Interaction provides learners with the information needed to manage the depth of study, range of content covered, type of alternative media needed for information presentations, and time actually spent on a specific learning task (Kinsey, 1990). McCombs (1992) notes that the depth and breadth of information processed, as well as what and how much is learned and remembered, are influenced by the following factors:

- Self-awareness and beliefs about personal control, competence, and ability
- Clarity and salience of personal values, interests, and goals
- Personal expectations for success and failure
- Affect, emotion, and general states of mind and the resulting motivation to learn

Interaction for learner control or self-regulation is particularly important within the context of preparing individuals to be lifelong learners, since it deals with the ability of a learner stay on task, to mediate the need for additional information to complete one's understanding, and to recognize when the learning task has been completed.

Interaction to increase motivation. McCombs (1992) observes that individuals are naturally curious and enjoy learning. However, they acknowledge that intense negative conditions and emotions (for example, feeling insecure; worrying about failure; being self-conscious or shy; or fearing corporal punishment, ridicule, or stigmatizing labels) can thwart this enthusiasm. The degree to which a learner can ascertain the presence or absence of these and other limiting factors will have a direct impact on his or her ability to learn. Therefore, interaction provides opportunities for making these determinations through asking questions, clarifying statements, reviewing guidelines, and so on.

Interaction for negotiation of understanding. Determining the willingness of another individual to engage in a dialogue, to come to consensus, or to agree to conform to terms of an agreement are all examples of interactions for negotiation. Negotiations in learning are particularly relevant in a time where constructivist learning models are used to explain how individuals can use their own (appropriate) interpretations of reality to enhance relevancy, motivation, and application. In addition, being able to clearly articulate and agree on the terms of a learning agreement increases the likelihood of achieving a successful outcome.

Interaction for team building. In order to understand the importance of interaction as a strategy for building a team, it is important to understand a bit about the dynamics of team development. Newell, Wagner, and Gerner (1988) observe that there are four stages of team development.

Membership, where individual members of a learning cohort or workgroup determine where they fit in the overall social and task structure of the group.
Subgroupings, where individuals identify with other individual team members to form associations and friendships, at times to the exclusion of others within the cohort or workgroup.
Confrontation, where individuals' behaviors disrupt the overall flow of collaboration and participation. This stage is characterized by an "us versus them" mentality that makes it difficult to achieve any collaborative group outcome.
Shared leadership, where disagreements occur but are focused more around tasks and issues than around individuals or subgroups of individuals. Individual uniqueness is valued, but no more than is the collective team effort. The team shares information easily, there is real commitment to meeting the goals of the group, and responsibility for achieving these goals is shared.

Interaction for team building is necessary to ensure that individual members of a team actively support the goals of the group. Interactions facilitate such desirable behaviors as recognition and acceptance of individual differences, expression of respect for the team as well as for its members, effective listening, a shared sense of responsibility, and the ability to confirm expectations within the group.

Interaction for discovery. "Pushing the envelope" is a phrase that captures the excitement of structuring information so that new interpretations of that information are enabled. It is highly unusual for new discoveries to occur in an intellectual vacuum. This category of interaction refers to the cross-fertilization of ideas that occurs when people share their ideas and perspectives with one another in the pursuit of defining new constructs.

Interaction for exploration. Closely related to "interaction for discovery," interaction for exploration provides a vehicle for defining the scope, depth, and breadth of a new idea. It is also important to distinguish a new idea from extant ideas. This category of interaction helps define the parameters within which such distinctions can be made.

Interaction for clarification of understanding. This relates to the ability to navigate one's way through a sea of performance expectations that may or may not be clearly articulated. An example of this category of interaction may include determining whether one's personal interpretation is what another person actually intended by restating expectations in one's own words.

Interaction for closure. Just as learners need to know where to begin a specific learning endeavor, they also need to know when they are done with the endeavor. In an era marked by access to almost limitless information resources, the ability to "bound" an activity is critical, whether one is writing a term paper or staying "in scope" on a contracted project. This means being able to determine what expectations exist and also to determine when those expectations have been met. It is a rare individual who can make these determinations without engaging in dialogue.

Applying Interaction in Practice

Using the categories of interaction noted above as conceptual benchmarks, it is fairly easy to make the case that interaction is a necessary ingredient for a quality learning experience. What is not so clear, at least not when interaction is viewed as an independent construct, is the value that interaction brings to a learning endeavor. For example, one might attempt to quantify the amount of interaction that is needed to ensure the quality of a learning experience. One may be interested in determining how often interaction should occur for a learning experience to be effective. There may even be some interest in determining what types of interaction are the most effective. However, it is hard to imagine that the result of any of these inquiries would offer any useful insights or understandings.

The best rule of thumb for effectively designing an interactive learning experience—whether it happens to be distance learning, on-line learning, or face-to-face, instructor-led learning experiences—is to first consider the goals and objectives of a specific learning experience. From this perspective, it is both far more appropriate and effective to begin the process of selecting the strategies and tactics needed to achieve the desired ends of the learning experience, for the specific audience at hand, given the specific conditions likely to be encountered in a given setting. In this way, interaction can serve as an outcome of clearly conceptualized, well-designed, and well-developed instruction and training.

References

Dede, C. "Emerging Technologies and Distributed Learning." *The American Journal of Distance Education,* 1997, *10* (2), 4–36.

Kinsey, M. B. "Requirements and Benefits of Effective Interactive Instruction: Learner Control, Self-Regulation, and Continuing Motivation." *Educational Technology Research and Development,* 1990, *38* (1), 5–21.

McCombs, B. L. *Learner-Centered Psychological Principles: Guidelines for School Redesign and Reform.* Washington, D.C.: American Psychological Association and the Mid-Continent Regional Education Laboratory, 1992.

Moore, M. G. "Three Modes of Interaction. A Presentation of the NUCEA Forum: Issues in Instructional Interactivity." Presented at annual meeting of National University Continuing Education Association, Salt Lake City, Utah, April 1989.

Newell, K., Wagner, E. D., and Gerner, M. "Team-Building for Better Decision Making and Problem Solving." *Performance and Instruction,* 1988, *27* (8), 11–16.

Wagner, E. D. "In Support of a Function Definition of Interaction." *The American Journal of Distance Education,* 1994, *8* (20), 6–29.

ELLEN D. WAGNER is vice president of consulting services for Informania, Inc., San Francisco.

Visual thinking clarifies communication and enhances the learning process. One form of visual thinking, word pictures, will help distance instructors to clarify their presentations and provide students with visual outlines of the key points of a telelesson.

Visual Thinking: Let Them See What You Are Saying

Thomas E. Cyrs

"It's amazing what you can see by looking." "Do you see?" "It's in the mind's eye." "I wish I could see what you are saying." "A picture is worth a thousand words." These phrases are often used by students as they attend traditional lectures on college campuses across the country. However, when applied to teaching at a distance, they take on a new meaning that will affect the way we teach.

Students live in a society permeated with visual media, yet the primary means of communication in college classrooms is the spoken word in a lecture format. As electronic media become more common on campuses, we need to communicate in ways that complement that spoken lecture with visualizations.

Telecommunications, and especially television in its present analog form and increasingly available digital form, continually push toward higher levels of visual communication. Multimedia, which emphasizes visual communication, is fast approaching our classrooms. To hold the interest of the students of this visual society, distance learning instructors need to begin to think and present ideas visually. As digital technology merges voice, video, and data and integrates them all into multimedia, instructors must design new telecourses and modify existing ones to let students see as well as hear what they are saying.

Visual Thinking

Visual thinking is the ability to conceptualize and present thoughts, ideas, and data as pictures and graphics, replacing much of the verbiage we now use to communicate (Wileman, 1993). Visual thinking is a mode of thinking that is nonanalytic and nonalgorithmic. It is composed of three overlapping strategies of thought: imaging, seeing, and designing (Figure 4.1).

NEW DIRECTIONS FOR TEACHING AND LEARNING, no. 71, Fall 1997 © Jossey-Bass Publishers

Figure 4.1. Visual Thinking

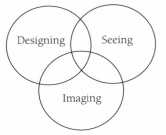

Seeing is the visual perception of two-or three-dimensional objects and the linking of these perceptions with the past experiences of the viewer. *Imaging* involves perceiving different roles for given objects and being aware of alter- native realities. For example, if we see a book, we know that its purpose is to convey a story or information in written and/or graphic form. Alternative roles for a book could be to serve as protection from rain, as a doorstop, or as a fly-swatter. *Designing* involves expressing an idea in some type of visual form, such as creating a sculpture or drawing a picture (Moses, 1982). Instructors can use all three strategies to communicate more effectively with students.

The use of visuals of any type can provide more concrete meaning to words and can show connections and relationships among ideas. Thornburg (1992, p. 51) notes, "The left-right, top-bottom world of Gutenberg has been joined by an explosion of non-linear and (in many cases) highly interactive information tools in the home." Much of this information is highly visualized and demands new ways of thinking other than the use of letter symbols grouped as abstract words. Visualizing our key ideas using visuals ranging from minimally detailed graphics to concrete, detailed pictures can provide more concrete meaning for the students than words alone.

Graphic Organizers

Almost all of the descriptors for visual displays fall under the rubric of graphic organizers of one type or another. Graphic organizers help students see relationships between key ideas more readily and economically than we can convey in words.

The theory underlying graphic organizers is that the visual and verbal organizational structure of a graphic diagram consolidates information into a meaningful whole so that students do not have the impression that they are being taught a series of unrelated facts or concepts. Graphic organizers have been referred to in the literature as structured overviews or tree diagrams (Barron, 1969); cognitive maps (Diekhoff and Diekhoff, 1982); outline graphics (Braden, 1982); and structured note-taking (Smith and Tompkins, 1988).

Graphic organizers are generally characterized by key words and phrases linked graphically to form a meaningful representation. They can help students see the interrelationships among ideas and how they are connected, speed up comprehension, improve note taking, and provide an idea storyboard not possible with linear, words-only lecture outlines. The figures used in this chapter could be considered graphic organizers in that they represent the relationships among the concepts being discussed.

Types of Visual Symbols

Three types of symbols are used in visual thinking, as shown in Figure 4.2. They include pictures, graphic symbols, and verbal symbols (Wileman, 1993). Verbal symbols represented as words only are the most common and most frequently used means of communication, yet are the most abstract. Pictures are the most accurate way to communicate but are often the most difficult, time-consuming, and expensive type of symbol to obtain. To employ a graphic artist to visualize ideas is the ideal solution, but few faculty have the funds for this. Fortunately, the advent of computer presentation software has provided one possible means of creating graphics that is minimally time-consuming and immediately available to any instructor with a minimum of experience: graphic symbols.

Graphic symbols consist of image-related graphics, concept-related graphics, and arbitrary graphics (see Figure 4.3).

Image-related graphics are highly recognizable representations of an object or idea and use such things as silhouettes, profiles on an object with detail, or computer or print clip art. In an image-related graphic of an apple, shading and detail would clearly identify it as an apple.

Concept-related graphics remove as much detail as possible and often stylize an object but still render it generally recognizable for what it is. Thus an apple, though greatly simplified as an outline, would still be recognizable as an apple.

Arbitrary graphics are abstract symbols conceived in an instructor's imagination as a way to show relationships among ideas. Figure 4.3 is an example of an arbitrary graphic called a word picture. It summarizes the key ideas of this paragraph, but as a stand-alone graphic would require further explanation. These graphics do not look like the things that they represent but are

Figure 4.2. Visual Symbols

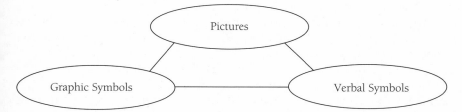

Figure 4.3. Types of Graphic Symbols

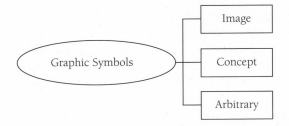

related logically and conceptually. Arbitrary graphics include geometric shapes, flowcharts, network maps, mind maps, and other schematic charts and diagrams. Arbitrary graphics are familiar to instructors and well within their ability to design simply and immediately.

Word Pictures

During a telelecture, graphic organizers present the logical conceptual outline for a presentation. A special simplified type of graphic organizer, called a *word picture,* has been designed for use on television and computer screens.

A *word picture* is a graphic representation composed of key concepts and ideas derived from the organizational patterns of a lecture. Key words and phrases are the most important concepts in a written or spoken statement and provide valuable clues to the level of importance of the content. The use of key words and phrases allows us to communicate with an economy of words in skeleton form. These ideas and concepts and the relationships between them are represented in geometric nodes using pictorial, graphic, and verbal symbols (Cyrs and Smith, 1990).

Word pictures can use a variety of graphics (pictures, photographs, clip art, geometric shapes, color, key words and numbers, stick figures, silhouettes, line art, underlining, or any symbolic technique) to represent a concept or idea. The key words and phrases are embedded in geometric shapes and linked with lines and arrows to show relationships among the ideas. A line means that some type of relationship or connection exists. Lines can also denote examples of a key idea. Arrows mean cause, product, result, or leads to. The node can contain key words or phrases or can stand alone as a representation of something that needs no further verbal explanation. Instructors new to the concept of word pictures usually start with arbitrary graphics such as geometric shapes with key words in simple, horizontally laid out word pictures and graduate to higher forms of concept- and image-related graphics as their visualization skills develop.

Word pictures are shown on a television or computer screen as the instructor develops a presentation. They are reproduced and numbered in student handouts that correspond with the same numbers on the screen, as shown in Figure 4.4, samples A and B. The key words can be left blank in the

Figure 4.4. Examples of Word Pictures

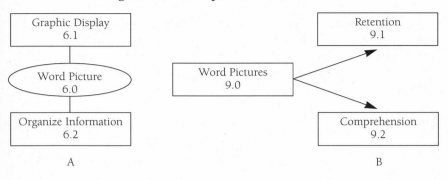

A

B

handout to be filled in by the student as the instructor presents each idea. In the case of audio conferencing, each part of a word picture is numbered and referenced as the audio presentation is delivered.

Visualizing Ideas from a Presentation

How does an instructor visualize ideas? Where will an instructor find ideas that are worthy of visualization? What can an instructor who is not very visual do to assist students to visualize key ideas? There are many sources of visual ideas that can be seen on television, in print media, in computer software, and in other commercial formats. Instructors should remain alert to the possibility of using these visualizations as prototypes for their own graphics. Becoming aware of the visualizations of ideas that surround us every day will sharpen the instructor's own visual sense.

When developing a telelesson, an instructor should limit a presentation to three or four key points during a fifty-minute teleclass. Given these key points, the instructor can then write out in narrative form or at least in tight outline form the presentation, regardless of length (written to be heard, not read by the student). This will provide a basis for searching out areas to visualize.

The instructor should underline or highlight indicators in the narrative worthy of visualization. These indicators can be found in such things as visual analogies; summaries; maps or lists; graphs, tables, and charts; comparisons and contrasts; colorful descriptions; people; time or sequence indicators; geography; comparative dimensions; and a host of other possibilities. The narrative will hold the key to concepts that lend themselves to visual depiction.

To visually depict these concepts, the instructor can draw on graphics software along with clip art, real pictures, cartoons, and all manner of standard shapes and forms. The sophistication of the depiction is often not as important as the simplicity and clarity of the relationships depicted. The important idea is to learn to draw as well as to explain the concepts being taught. By learning from observing others and not being afraid to experiment, an instructor can become quite proficient at visualizing his or her ideas almost as clearly as he or she can explain them.

Visual thinking skills will become more and more important as the newer delivery technologies for distance learning are integrated into new and converted telecourses. Without higher levels of visualization, instructors will perpetuate the "talking head" and "writing hand" so prevalent today in distance learning telecourses.

References

Barron, R. F. "The Use of Vocabulary as an Advanced Organizer." In H. L. Berber and P. L. Sanders (eds.), *Research in Reading the Content Areas: First Year Report.* Syracuse, N.Y.: Reading and Language Arts Center, University of Syracuse, 1969.

Braden, R. A. "Visualizing the Verbal and Verbalizing the Visual." Paper presented at the annual conference of the International Visual Literacy Association, Vancouver, British Columbia, 1982.

Cyrs, T., and Smith, F. A. *Teleclass Teleteaching: A Resource Guide.* (2nd ed.) Las Cruces: Center for Educational Development, New Mexico State University, 1990.

Diekhoff, G. M., and Diekhoff, K. B. "Cognitive Maps as a Tool in Communicating Structural Knowledge." *Educational Technology,* 1982, *11* (4), 28–30.

Moses, B. "Visualization: A Different Approach to Problem Solving." *School Science and Mathematics,* 1982, *82* (2), 141–147.

Smith, P. L., and Tompkins, G. E. "Structured Notetaking: A New Strategy for Content Area Readers." *Journal of Reading,* 1988, *34,* 46–53.

Thornburg, D. O. *Edutrends 2010: Restructuring, Technology, and the Future of Education.* New York: Starsong Publications, 1992.

Wileman, R. E. *Visual Communicating.* Englewood Cliffs, N.J.: Educational Technology Publications, 1993.

THOMAS E. CYRS is professor of educational management and development in the College of Education and the senior faculty adviser for teaching in the Center for Educational Development at New Mexico State University. He is also president of Educational Development Associates.

This chapter describes student-centered learning and the variables associated with optimal learning and provides suggestions for designing student-centered telecourses for college students and adult learners.

Student-Centered Instruction for the Design of Telecourses

M. Winston Egan, Gordon S. Gibb

Telecourse instruction should be designed to promote student learning and related outcomes. Recent and past research reviews of television instruction demonstrate that students perform as well on outcome measures in television courses as they do in traditional courses (Chu and Schramm, 1975; Whittington, 1987). The question is not whether television can serve as a useful medium for delivering instruction, but what instructional elements and approaches make television instruction effective (Whittington, 1987). Specifically, what learner variables and teaching strategies need to be considered in promoting and achieving positive outcomes for telecourse students?

This chapter describes student-centered instruction for telecourses and provides a rationale for this kind of instruction. Additionally, the chapter presents important information about variables that contribute to student learning and gives suggestions for designing learner-centered instruction for telecourses that maximizes these variables. The chapter concludes with a summary of suggestions for delivering student-centered instruction through telecourses.

Student Learning Variables and Design Implications for Telecourses

Researchers have identified student learning variables that contribute to effective and meaningful learning in college students and adult learners (Angelo, 1993; Ference and Vockell, 1994; Forsyth and McMillan, 1991; Morgan, 1991).

Student-centered instruction is clear and understandable (Lowman, 1984), is responsive to the ways in which students learn and communicate (Kolb, 1984), acknowledges students' interest and motivations (Forsyth and

McMillan, 1991), and honors the social nature of learning (Johnson, Johnson, and Smith, 1991). Additionally, it is engaging (Bonwell and Eison, 1991) and focuses on the explicit needs of learners for meaningful and timely feedback (Van Houten, 1980).

Achieving Clarity Through Organization and Planning. Instructors whose teaching is clear and easy to understand provide distinct examples of ideas and concepts, point out topic transitions, and consistently identify key points (Pascarella and Terenzini, 1994). At least one study suggests that instructor clarity accounts for as much as 52 percent of the variance in mean class achievement (Hines, Cruickshank, and Kennedy, 1982).

Telecourse instructors achieve clarity by creating detailed, precise syllabi and interactive study guides (Cyrs and Smith, 1992). These syllabi and study guides are often broader in scope and more specific in content than those prepared for conventional courses. Some instructors refer to this combination of materials as "extended syllabi."

In particular, interactive study guides are designed to counter the "couch potato" phenomenon: They are structured to move students from passive reception to active learning and engagement during telecourse sessions. Additionally, they provide students with visual representations of knowledge structures, intricate processes, and other complex phenomena. Another benefit of these guides is the assistance they give to students in managing the flow of information presented during telecourses and in understanding the relationships between concepts or processes. Extended syllabi are designed to compensate for the absence of informal instructor/student interactions that would typically take place before, during, or after conventional course sessions. Extended syllabi also help students know exactly how to proceed with course assignments, how to make the most of each telecourse session, how to prepare successfully for examinations, how to develop and submit assignments of quality, and how to monitor personal progress in completing telecourses.

Another crucial aspect of clarity is achieved through planning clear objectives and related learning activities for each course session. Advanced preparation and planning are essential. Television teaching, by its very nature, is a team process, frequently involving several other professionals in developing and delivering instruction. Instructors who are accustomed to planning their instruction several hours before they enter their conventional classrooms and who use these same habits of preparation for telecourses will disappoint themselves and their telecourse students. Successful telecourse instruction requires much more extensive planning and collaborative work with other professionals than does conventional instruction.

Clarity is also achieved through careful selection of course content. Rather than "covering" course content, effective telecourse instructors work at uncovering difficult-to-understand concepts and themes. They do this by directing their teaching and learning activities to concepts that would be difficult for most students to understand on their own. Additionally, these instructors segment their sessions into manageable and interesting sections. Cyrs and Smith

(1992) have often referred to these sections as "lecturettes." These lecturettes are generally followed by activity-oriented student tasks. Like typical sequences of the television news, these learning segments are a mix of explanations, illustrations, and questions. However, unlike the news, telecourse students are required to engage in some activity that ensures their learning. Learning activities may be done individually, in dyads, or in small learning teams at each receiving site.

Carefully selected graphics, engaging video segments, and other computer-generated animations can also contribute to clarity. Unfortunately, many instructors are not accustomed to thinking or communicating visually and do not understand how to utilize fully the visual strengths of television. However, with appropriate support from instructional designers, graphic artists, and other visually oriented production personnel, instructors may learn how to use television to heighten the clarity and engagement of their instruction.

Assessing Prior Knowledge and Orientation to Learning. Telecourse designers need to know their students. Wagner (1993, p. 29) refers to this as "audience analysis." This analysis includes assessing students' entry-level knowledge or skills, their motivations for taking the telecourse(s), their course-related interests and fears, their prior experience with telecourses, and their preferred means for processing information and responding to assignments. Specific information may be gathered from students before or during the first week of the telecourse through student surveys, pretests, and other data sources provided by the institution offering the telecourses. Student surveys might include the following questions:

What are your reasons for taking telecourses?
What are your personal learning goals when taking a telecourse?
What are your greatest fears about completing telecourses successfully?
What instructor behaviors and teaching approaches make a difference in your learning?
What telecourse features (student study groups, well-designed course session guides, computer listserv or bulletin board, e-mail, and so on) significantly contribute to your learning?

Responses to these and other questions provide telecourse development teams, particularly instructors, with valuable information about planning learning experiences, selecting specific teaching strategies, organizing study groups, developing review sessions, and structuring telecourse assignments. Additionally, this kind of information affects the types of examples used in lessons, the approaches taken in assessing student performance, the kinds of assignments given, and even the kinds of humor that may be employed during the telecourse sessions.

Stimulating Motivation in Students. Intrinsic motivation generally hinges on students' curiosity (McKeachie, 1986), their desire to achieve, their expectations of success, and their goals for learning (Forsyth and McMillan,

1991). Curiosity is aroused by stimuli that are novel but not so different as to be incongruous with prior knowledge or experience (McKeachie, 1986). Regardless of whether the telecourse is live or taped, the instructor must introduce novelty in several ways: asking unexpected questions that cause students to analyze their prior knowledge in new ways; providing brief start-up activities in which students predict the relationships between prior knowledge and new content; introducing case studies as vehicles for making sense of new content; interjecting "pair and share" activities in which students briefly work with partners to answer questions, make predictions, or summarize new information; and ending each class session with a curiosity-arousing preview of the next session.

Students' goals for learning and their expectations of success are also important motivators. Instructors should begin each course by asking students to use the course syllabus to define their goals for learning and to outline what responsibility they will take to achieve these goals. Students may also set benchmarks for progress to be evaluated at regular intervals. Instructors should then provide feedback throughout the telecourse so that students continue to be motivated by their progress and achievement.

Developing Learning Communities. Distance learners, by definition, are not in the immediate presence of their instructors, so essential interactions between teachers and students that help clarify information are crucial. It is therefore important that instructors facilitate the organization of learning communities (Verduin and Clark, 1991).

Learning communities are groups of students who meet face to face or through electronic means. These groups provide opportunities for students to teach one another, to clarify course-related questions and assignments, to receive academic and social support, and to develop relationships that extend beyond the duration of telecourses.

Telecourse instructors and designers promote learning communities by creating reliable means by which learners may interact face to face and at a distance. Face-to-face interactions may be fostered by forming study groups. As students register for telecourses, they are encouraged to sign up for study groups in their geographic areas. Students simply give permission to instructors to share their names and telephone numbers with other students who have similar interests and concerns. Some students may volunteer to host study groups. Another approach for connecting students is the establishment of a listserv or electronic bulletin board. This kind of connection allows students and instructors to interact freely through e-mail. Questions, responses, or comments may be shared by e-mail with all course participants, several participants, or just one student. Also, instructors may use the listserv for informal interactions with students. Conference calls can also be used to connect individuals in telecourses. Conference calls provide a means for students and instructors to gather by telephone for discussion groups, test reviews, or other telecourse activities.

Employing Teacher Immediacy Behaviors to Foster Interaction. *Teacher immediacy* behaviors (Sanders and Wiseman, 1994) are essential to good telecourse instruction. These are instructor behaviors that invite interaction, suggest approachability, and foster positive affective outcomes in students. Course designers assist instructors by encouraging them to learn and use students' names, to vary their vocal expressiveness, to smile with appropriate frequency, and to establish eye contact with students at a distance by frequently relating to the television cameras. These behaviors contribute positively to students' feelings about their learning and to the efforts students devote to telecourse activities and assignments.

Using Active Learning to Promote Student Engagement. Unfortunately, much of what is offered through telecourses is the "talking head," or lecture-based teaching. Research regarding this teaching approach and its effectiveness in promoting quality learning is not encouraging (Bonwell and Eison, 1991; Johnson, Johnson, and Smith, 1991; Meyers and Jones, 1993). *Active learning* involves more than listening, being alert, and paying attention. It consists of being actively involved in discussing problems, seeking solutions to case studies or dilemmas, responding to simulations, participating in games, and making decisions.

Telecourse development teams should create learning experiences that promote engagement rather than passivity. To do so they must carefully consider the objectives of the telecourse, the nature of the subject matter, and the capabilities of the students and the instructor. Several prominent researchers and practitioners have provided recommendations for moving students from passive to active learning habits. The recommendations center on creating *interactive study guides* (Cyrs and Smith, 1991); developing critical thinking skills through debate teams, critical incidents, dramatizations, and scenario building (Jones and Safrit, 1994); employing embedded questions for immediate student responses in video-anchored presentations (Cennamo, Savenye, and Smith, 1991); applying alternative formats for lectures (Bonwell and Eison, 1991); and using cooperative learning groups (Johnson, Johnson, and Smith, 1991).

Using Feedback to Promote Learning. Feedback is essential for students to create meaning from that which they have learned. Students develop as learners when appropriate feedback alerts them to the accuracy of their work and deters them from learning things that may have to be unlearned later (Angelo, 1993; Van Houten, 1980). Often students decide whether they will stay with a telecourse based on the feedback received on an initial assignment and/or exam. If the feedback is late, not very specific, and inappropriate to students' entry-level skills or knowledge, they may withdraw from the telecourse or commit less energy to it (Egan, Ferraris, Jones, and Sebastian, 1993).

Depending on the course technology, timely and efficient feedback can be accomplished by e-mail, two-way audio/video, telephone, fax, or mail. Tutors, on-site facilitators, and graders can be used to reduce the time between submission and return of assignments.

Feedback is also critical for instructors. An example of helpful course feedback is a simple *Stop, Start, and Continue Request Form*. On this form, students are simply asked to identify behaviors or procedures that an instructor should stop, start, or continue.

Conclusion

Those designing student-centered instruction for telecourses must consider the variables that contribute to meaningful and motivated student learning that have been discussed in this chapter. While many of these ideas are just as useful for regular classroom instruction, they are particularly important in a distance situation. Unlike much conventional instruction, telecourse teaching is generally an intensive and often demanding team process requiring more extensive planning and coordination among professionals constituting the design team. If the telecourse instructors take the time to build in the clarity, connections, teacher immediacy behaviors, and active learning we have described, their telecourses will be truly student centered and oriented toward appropriate outcomes.

References

Angelo, T. "Fourteen General, Research Based Principles for Improving Higher Education." *AAHE Bulletin,* 1993, *45* (8), 5–7.

Bonwell, C. C., and Eison, J. A. *Active Learning: Creating Excitement in the Classroom.* ASHE/ERIC report. Washington, D.C.: School of Education and Human Development, George Washington University, 1991.

Cennamo, K. S., Savenye, W. C., and Smith, P. "Mental Effort and Video-Based Learning: The Relationship of Preconceptions and the Effects of Interactive and Covert Practice." *Education Technology Research and Development,* 1991, *39* (1), 5–16.

Chu, G., and Schramm, W. *Learning from Television: What the Research Says,* Washington, D.C.: National Association of Educational Broadcasting, 1975. (ED 109 985)

Cyrs, T. E., and Smith, F. A. "Designing Interactive Study Guides with Word Pictures for Teleclass Teaching." *TechTrends,* 1991, *36* (1), 37–39.

Cyrs, T. E., and Smith, F. A. *Essential Skills for Television Teaching: There Is a Difference.* Las Cruces: Center for Educational Development, College of Human and Community Services, New Mexico State University, 1992.

Egan, M. W., Ferraris, C., Jones, D. E., and Sebastian, J. "The Telecourse Experience: A Student Perspective." *Education Journal,* 1993, *7* (5), j1–j7.

Ference, P. R., and Vockell, E. L. "Adult Learning Characteristics and Effective Software Instruction." *Educational Technology,* 1994, *34* (60), 25–31.

Forsyth, D. R., and McMillan, J. H. "Practical Proposals for Motivating Students." In R. Menges and M. Svinicki (eds.), *College Teaching: From Theory to Practice.* New Directions for Teaching and Learning, no. 34. San Francisco: Jossey-Bass, 1991.

Hines, C., Cruickshank, D., and Kennedy, J. "Measures of Teacher Clarity and Their Relationships to Student Achievement and Satisfaction." Paper presented at the annual meeting of the American Educational Research Association, New York, 1982.

Johnson, D. W., Johnson, R. T., and Smith, K. A. *Active Learning: Cooperation in the College Classroom.* Edina, Minn.: Interaction Book Company, 1991.

Jones, J. M., and Safrit, R. D. "Developing Critical Thinking Skills in Adult Learners Through Innovative Distance Learning." Report no. CE 066957. Jinan, China: International Conference on the Practice of Adult Education and Social Development, 1994. (ED 373 159)

Kolb, D. A. *Experiential Learning: Experience as the Source of Learning and Development.* Englewood Cliffs, N.J.: Prentice Hall, 1984.

Lowman, J. *Mastering the Techniques of Teaching.* San Francisco: Jossey-Bass, 1984.

McKeachie, W. J. *Teaching Tips: A Guidebook for the Beginning College Teacher.* (8th ed.) Lexington, Mass.: Heath, 1986.

Meyers, C., and Jones, T. B. *Promoting Active Learning: Strategies for the College Classroom.* San Francisco: Jossey-Bass, 1993.

Morgan, A. "Research into Student Learning in Distance Education." Victoria, Australia: Deakin University, 1991. (ED 342 371)

Pascarella, E. T., and Terenzini, P. T. "How College Affects Students." In K. A. Feldman and M. B. Paulsen (eds.), *Teaching and Learning in the College Classroom.* Needham Heights, Mass.: Ginn Press, 1994.

Sanders, J. A., and Wiseman, R. L. "The Effects of Verbal and Nonverbal Teacher Immediacy on Perceived Cognitive, Affective, and Behavioral Learning in the Multicultural Classroom." In K. A. Feldman and M. B. Paulsen (eds.), *Teaching and Learning in the College Classroom.* Needham Heights, Mass.: Ginn Press, 1994.

Van Houten, R. *Learning Through Feedback: A Systematic Approach for Improving Academic Performance.* New York: Human Services, 1980.

Verduin, J. R., and Clark, T. A. *Distance Education: The Foundations of Effective Practice.* San Francisco: Jossey-Bass, 1991.

Wagner, E. D. "Variables Affecting Distance Educational Program Success." *Educational Technology,* 1993, *33* (4), 28–32.

Whittington, N. "Is Instructional Television Educationally Effective? A Research Review." *American Journal of Distance Education,* 1987, *1* (1), 47–57.

M. WINSTON EGAN *and* GORDON S. GIBB *are both members of the Department of Educational Psychology at Brigham Young University.*

Distance learners are in need of as much attention as their instructors.
This chapter recommends areas to consider in supporting their
learning.

Learner Development: Beyond the Technology

Darcy Walsh Hardy, Mary H. Boaz

Distance educators have produced many research studies focused on technology (media comparison studies) and, recently, on such areas as faculty development and instructional design (Moore and Thompson, 1990; Olcott and Wright, 1995; Hardy, Abiatti, and Ashcroft, 1995; Clark, 1987; Koumi, 1994). Studies have also looked at student issues such as learning styles and completion rates, but few have turned their attention to student development in distance education. This chapter presents the results of the study of these issues and, perhaps more importantly, an outline for creating student development materials for distance education programs.

What is meant by student development? For our purpose, the term refers to the preparation of the student for a distance education experience, beyond the technical orientation. While many programs train faculty for distance teaching, students in distance education are rarely given such an opportunity. They simply appear on the first day of class, receive a technical overview and a few handouts, and begin class. The students begin the course at a disadvantage due to the lack of information they receive, unlike traditional on-campus students.

When students enroll in traditional face-to-face courses, they generally have access to a plethora of documents intended to prepare them for the learning experience. These documents may include the institution's catalogue, the individual department's information packet, and specific information related to student support services.

On the other hand, students who enroll in a distance learning course may or may not receive the sponsoring institution's catalogue. Even if they do receive a catalogue, very few catalogues currently include information about what to expect as a distance student. Often the distance student is aware of the delivery mode but not of the complexities of the technology or logistics involved.

These discrepancies between information and support offered to traditional on-campus students and that offered to distance students provided the impetus for this study. Hoping to gain a clearer picture of student development in distance education, we distributed a survey that asked questions related to the kind of pre-course and in-class support students receive from the sending institution and its faculty. While support services such as library access, Internet accounts, and advising were included in the survey, our focus remains on student preparation for the distance learning experience and precisely who is responsible for providing this preparation.

Burge and Howard (1988) conducted an attitudinal study involving experienced practitioners in the field of distance teaching. Overall, the respondents were very positive regarding the importance of "learner-centered" education experiences but noted that this focus had some disadvantages and that students should be encouraged to "take responsibility for their progress in learning, but it is not something that most students are capable of doing right away" (p. 14). Burge and Howard offer the following conclusion: "What does emerge from comments [in the surveys] is a recognition of the complexity of the educational process, in particular for distance education modes of delivery, and the knowledge that responsibility in this enterprise is shared among all participants" (p. 17).

While students must be responsible for many of the issues facing them during their collegiate years, the distance student faces additional challenges. It is almost a *requirement* that distance students be more focused, better time managers, and able to work both independently and as group members, depending on the delivery mode and location of the distance course (Gibson, 1996). Other characteristics required for distance learning include strong self-motivation, self-discipline, and assertiveness. The question raised here, however, is whether students know what is expected of them in the distance learning environment. Finally, if it is important to assist these students in their preparation, whose responsibility is it?

The Survey

In the spring of 1996, a survey instrument was developed by the authors and distributed by electronic and traditional means (mail and in-class dissemination). The survey consisted of five sections: Student Profile, Administrative Issues, Technical Issues, Access/Interaction, and Course Content/Interaction. The survey consisted of twenty questions, many of which were open-ended to allow for further explanations of responses. The survey specifically asked students if they felt the administration at the sending end of the course understood their needs as distance students.

Students were also asked to identify what information they were given and what information they felt should be added to better prepare them for the distance learning experience. Nearly two hundred surveys were returned via mail, e-mail, and fax from across the country and from as far away as Australia. Respondents were involved in distance education via a variety of delivery methods, from print to videoconferencing.

Results

The results of the student surveys indicate that not enough is being done to ensure success in a distance learning course. The following discussion of the results includes

• Demographics of the student respondents
• Students' feelings about the sending institution
• Student needs for successful distance learning experience

The Adult Learner and the Sending Institution. Demographics regarding the students who responded to the survey are consistent with those cited by Moore and Kearsley (1996) as typical of distance learning students. Respondents are primarily between the ages of twenty-five and fifty. Almost two-thirds are female, most are married, and the majority are working full-time while taking courses. This information, when combined with Knowles's (1978) principles of the adult learner, is closely related to the characteristics and principles of learner centeredness (listed below) as identified by Brandes and Ginnis (Burge and Howard, 1988). The adult learner generally meets these criteria and often demands that the principles be followed in the learning experience.

• The learner has full responsibility for her own learning.
• The subject matter has relevance and meaning for the learner.
• Involvement and participation are necessary for learning.
• The relationship between learners shows helping styles and learner self-responsibility.
• The teacher is a facilitator and resource person.
• The learner sees himself differently as a result of the learning experience.
• The learner experiences confluences (Burge and Howard, 1988, p. 2).

If the majority of adult distance learners fit the above criteria, a critical question in the survey is, "Do you feel the administration at the 'sending' end demonstrates an understanding of your needs as a distance student?" Although a number of students responded positively to this question, those who did not indicated that their institutions failed to provide the support stated by the positive respondents. Certainly, the most common complaint made by the negative respondents relates to nontechnical issues such as material distribution, overall communication, financial considerations, and knowledge of the institutions' policies and procedures.

Students commented that materials often arrived late or not at all. Others received their materials by fax, which was unreadable. Students were equally frustrated with the process of sending in assignments. One student enrolled in a real-time video class said that even though her assignments had to be turned in *prior* to the assignment due date in order to allow for mailing time, she received the graded lesson *after* the on-site students had received theirs.

The second most cited response to this question concerned communication in general. Many students apparently do not feel that there is quality communication between themselves and the sending campus. One student commented, "Sometimes, I think they don't know I'm alive. Do they care if I complete this course or not?" The lack of communication between the sending campus and the remote site often leads to a variety of problems, including failure to complete the course. These students do not know who to contact when technological problems occur or materials do not arrive on time.

Financial situations encountered by remote students can also be confusing. Many students who study completely by distance must still pay on-campus fees, such as activity fees, transportation, and student ID fees. In addition, students are often unaware of the financial aid options available to them. Most are under the impression that studying at a distance or enrolling at multiple institutions would render them ineligible for financial aid.

Overall, trying to maneuver around in the institution's bureaucracy can be especially frustrating for students studying at a distance. The amount of time and effort needed to reach the desired department can be overwhelming. Several students in the survey commented that even when they found the right person to talk to, they were treated as "second-class citizens" since they were not taking classes on the campus. Finally, one student summarized these issues by stating that too much is assumed (by the sending institution) about life in the "virtual classroom." Perhaps the first principle in learner centeredness should be expanded to read "The learner has full responsibility for her own learning *and logistics.*"

Registration and Related Issues. Another question in the survey asked, "What information could have been given to assist you with admission, registration, textbook sales, etc.?" The respondents overwhelmingly indicated a need to have textbooks available for sale at the remote sites (rather than at the campus bookstore or via mail order). In addition, students suggested not only that the textbooks be made available at remote sites, but also that an adviser or counselor assist with course selection. Many distance students do not receive information that on-site students typically receive, such as suggested course sequences or listings of future courses to be offered. They are often unaware of whom to contact for assistance with course selection unless they have taken at least one of their classes on campus.

The survey also asked about the issue of providing a handbook of information for distance students. The students' responses to this question shed light on what students actually need to be successful in the course beyond technical orientations, registration issues, and textbook problems. Students want a variety of additional information *before* the class begins. Information related to registration, faculty advising, and a list of additional courses available by distance is helpful, but students also need to know how to access services available to them from the main campus, as well as what will be expected of them in the distance learning environment. Students benefit most when they receive timely, consistent, noncontradictory information from the sending institution. Cyrs and Smith (1990) suggest a *telesyllabus,* an expanded syllabus that includes a technical explanation as well as administrative data.

Faculty information is critical to distance students. Since most students are unable to visit the main campus, they should be provided with phone numbers and e-mail addresses for their instructor, teaching assistants, and technical support personnel. A schedule of course topics and dates, deadlines for homework assignments, and a sample of World Wide Web sources for tracking additional information were suggested for inclusion in a student handbook. The students also want to see a listing of the main campus schedule, including official drop dates, final exam schedules, and important phone numbers (registrar, computer-help desk, financial aid, and so on). Extensive information related to the technical aspects of the course should be included, such as troubleshooting phone numbers both locally and at the originating site.

Student Needs. Several students identified a need to know more about what is expected of them in a distance course. Prospective students need to know that a distance course requires self-discipline, self-motivation, the ability to work independently, and perseverance. Information concerning interaction in the distance course should also be provided. Most students surveyed indicated a preference to be able interrupt the instruction in order to ask a question but did not know that this technique was appropriate or permitted.

In order to prepare the students for any type of interaction in the classroom, an information piece that identifies appropriate ways to question an instructor and how to interact with the rest of the class should be provided. McHenry and Bozik (1995) studied interaction at a distance and concluded that it is critical to the success of a learner in both face-to-face instruction and distance learning. Therefore, they recommend that instructors integrate interaction in their instruction by encouraging student interaction and supporting the proper use of equipment so that every student at each site may participate in classroom activities to the fullest.

Finally, students need to know how to deal with visits to the main campus, where appropriate. Maps, names, and phone numbers would assist these students who are able to come to campus on occasion. Because distance students often feel a loss of connection with the main campus, efforts should be made to provide a more inclusive atmosphere in the distance environment. Information posted to traditional students must be made available to distance students, either through a case-by-case approach or through a network. Policies that normally apply to traditional students may or may not apply to distance students. It is therefore critical to provide all relevant information to the students enrolled at a distance via a student handbook or by some other effective means of delivery.

Recommendations

The survey results described here, as well as those not discussed, lead us to make the following recommendations for learner development in distance education. Broadly, these recommendations relate to awareness, efficiency, and recognition.

Awareness. In Baker's *Tips for Being a Successful Distance Student* (1995), she suggests that distance learners should be more assertive in interrupting or "correcting" their instructor when he or she misuses the technology, even though this may be uncomfortable at first. Instructors must establish trust with distance learners by being open and honest regarding their level of skill with the technology, using humor to diffuse student anxiety. Instructors need to set ground rules during the first class meeting. Encouraging assertive behaviors by recognizing student interruptions and correcting audio and video problems as they are brought to the instructor's attention will serve the distance instructor and student both.

Efficiency. The majority of distance learners are adults with full-time work schedules and family responsibilities with limited time for academic activities. These students appreciate the effort to streamline the admission, scheduling, and advising processes to permit "one-stop shopping." This study and others (Moore, 1995; Workman and Stenard, 1996) reveal the importance of site coordinators to provide such streamlined support as advising, liaison to the main campus, and troubleshooting—for both technical and administrative problems.

Recognition. Distance students find it difficult to identify with the institution. University personnel often perpetuate this distance image by identifying students primarily by the communities in which they live and only secondarily as college students. Some institutions seem to make more of an effort to keep in touch with distant alumni than with distance students. For example, Workman and Stenard (1996) propose the simple solution of issuing university identification cards. In their study, students noted many uses for the ID cards: library access, discounts from merchants, and easier entry to facilities when visiting the main campus.

Conclusion

Many things can be done to assist the learner in a distance classroom setting. However, a question of responsibility may be raised at this point. Is the institution responsible for providing all of the above-mentioned services and information, or should the student be responsible for acquiring this knowledge?

This question was posed to the participants at a recent workshop we conducted. Most felt that it is indeed the sending institution's responsibility to provide information, access, and other services to the distance student. They also agreed that it is not in the best interest of the student nor within the means of the institutions' resources to simply replicate the on-campus experiences in smaller doses to the distance student. Instead, it is more appropriate to weave the distance education experience into the culture of the institution. All can then benefit from better access, greater flexibility, and a wider range of support services.

As a result of the survey discussed in this chapter and of comments received at the above-mentioned workshop, the following outline is recommended as a minimum amount of information to be distributed to distance learners.

Institutional issues
    Fee structures
    Policies for students studying at a distance
Logistics (pre-class information)
    Brief description of technology utilized
    Administrative information (admissions, advising, registration, textbooks)
    Personnel contact list for main campus and remote sites
    Listing of support services
    Sequence of courses leading to a degree (if applicable)
Academic
    Expanded course syllabus (telesyllabus)
    Grading policies, including deadlines for distance students
Suggested characteristics for distance learners
    Assertive
    Independent
    Self-disciplined
    Motivated

As can be seen from the above outline, these suggestions are merely the tip of the proverbial iceberg. The issues facing distance learners and those who provide programs for them are many. We encourage readers to use this material and continue the quest for providing distance learners with necessary information that will lead to a higher success rate for distance programs. As a result of efforts such as this, distance educators will be one step closer to truly meeting the needs of the growing population of learners at a distance.

References

Baker, M. H. "Tips for Being a Successful Distance Student." Handout distributed at post-conference workshop, 11th Annual Conference on Distance Teaching and Learning, Madison, Wis., August 1995.

Burge, E., and Howard, J. "Learner Centredness: Views of Canadian Distance Education Educators." Unpublished manuscript, Ontario Institute for Studies in Education, 1988.

Clark, R. E. "Which Technology for What Purpose? The State of the Argument About Research on Learning from Media." Paper presented at the Annual Convention of the Association for Educational Communications and Technology, Atlanta, Ga., 1987.

Cyrs, T. E., and Smith, F. A. *Teleclass Teaching: A Resource Guide.* (2nd ed.) Las Cruces: Center for Educational Development, New Mexico State University, 1990.

Gibson, C. C. "Toward an Understanding of Self-Concept in Distance Education." *American Journal of Distance Education,* 1996, *10* (1), 23–36.

Hardy, D. W., Abiatti, M., and Ashcroft, J. C. "Motion Curricula and Non-Motion Curricula in Distance Education: Technology Selection Reconsidered." *Canadian Journal of Educational Communication,* 1995, *24* (2), 105–115.

Knowles, M. S. *The Adult Learner.* Houston: Gulf Publishing, 1978.

Koumi, J. "Media Comparison and Deployment: A Practitioner's View." *British Journal of Educational Technology,* 1994, *25* (1), 41–57.

McHenry, L., and Bozik, M. "Communicating at a Distance: A Study of Interaction in a Distance Education Classroom." *Communication Education,* 1995, *44,* 362–370.

Moore, M. G. "The Five C's of the Local Coordinator." *American Journal of Distance Education,* 1995, *9* (1), 1–5.

Moore, M. G., and Kearsley, G. *Distance Education: A Systems View.* Belmont, CA: Wadsworth, 1996.

Moore, M. G., and Thompson, M. M. *The Effects of Distance Learning: A Review of the Literature.* Research monograph no. 2. University Park: American Center for the Study of Distance Education, Pennsylvania State University, 1990.

Olcott, D. J., and Wright, S. J. "An Institutional Framework for Increasing Faculty Participation in Postsecondary Distance Education." *American Journal of Distance Education,* 1995, *9* (3), 5–17.

Workman, J. J., and Stenard, R. A. "Student Support Services for Distance Learners." *ED, Education at a Distance,* 1996, *7,* 18–22.

DARCY WALSH HARDY is assistant director for distance education, Center for Instructional Technologies, The University of Texas at Austin.

MARY H. BOAZ is extended campus coordinator, Extended Campus Center at Paducah, Murray State University, in Kentucky.

Part Three

Alternative Delivery Systems for Distance Learning

Television teaching is the most popular distance learning medium today. Instructors experienced in the traditional classroom face significant challenges when entering this new teaching environment.

Teaching by Television

Virginia A. Ostendorf

Live video instruction is the fastest-growing distance learning delivery mode in the United States today (Ostendorf, 1996). More classes of students are being taught through this technology than by any other electronic medium. Although computer networks receive lots of attention in the media, in reality very few students receive formal class instruction, either credit or noncredit, via personal computer with modem. Even highly touted desktop conferencing is being adopted by many organizations largely because it allows an instructor to teach groups of students via live video and in real time. Although the information highway is used by many individuals for research and entertainment, that infobahn is still more a library than a classroom. The live delivery of instruction to groups, not to individuals, remains the norm whether learners gather face to face or are linked by electronic means.

Those instructors who wish to secure a place in the classroom of the future must first understand these technologies and the environment they are about to enter. They must step from the traditional classroom into the video world, accepting and adapting to its unique requirements.

What does it take to teach successfully by television? First, it is critically important to understand how distance learning differs from both commercial television and the traditional classroom. Preconceived notions about television and established practices in traditional teaching can be a great impediment when making the transition to television. It is far different from teaching in the traditional classroom. Unless we understand what we are trying to achieve by using these new systems, it is highly unlikely that we will be able to accomplish it.

Next, the instructor must be introduced in a general way to the basic technology to be employed, and to the specific role the instructor plays in the delivery of instruction. Not all distance learning video systems use the same technology or the same equipment; similarly, the role of the instructor also varies greatly by system.

Third, course design must take into consideration the system capabilities, the demographics of participating learners, and the electronic tools available to execute the design. But above all, it must demonstrate a bias for direct learner involvement and participation throughout the lesson. While lesson design is not the focus here, it should be assumed that whoever develops the course for delivery is experienced and knowledgeable in the demands of the medium.

Next comes training and practice to achieve mastery of each individual teaching tool. Only when each piece of equipment can be operated effortlessly will the instructor be free to focus on the subject matter at hand and on individual student needs in particular.

Finally, the instructor must master unique facilitation skills to assure that all remote learners can participate in interaction and other involvement activities equitably and with ease.

When all these elements have been addressed, the experienced classroom instructor can begin teaching by television.

Not Commercial Television

Too many instructors think teaching by television means presenting a performance or emulating a game show host. In fact, the opposite is true. A closer look at the basic premises of commercial television reveals that they directly contradict what is essential for excellence in distance teaching.

Commercial television focuses—literally and figuratively—on what takes place in the studio, to the complete exclusion of what occurs on the other side of the glass. Television producers put much time and effort into selecting what they call "the talent"; they attempt to engage only the most beautiful, vivacious, energetic, and engaging people to put on camera. They create elaborate sets, fuss with lighting and microphones, and choreograph in detail the length of segments and the sequence of events.

But what of the recipient of all this activity? The television viewer is literally that—one who views the actions and activities of others. No criteria whatsoever exist for those who will be the recipients of television programming. Even when token interaction is incorporated into television, viewer opinions are screened, presented in as short a time as possible, and then ignored. In the world of television, the ideal viewer has a pulse and a heartbeat, and little else. Commercial television is a one-sided playing field with all elements of production favoring the studio and those within it.

On the other hand, distance learning can succeed only when the remote learner is at the center of everything. Instructors are chosen for their subject mastery and delivery skills for the benefit of the learner. Visual materials are developed for maximum legibility and clarity for the benefit of the learner. Course design is based on activity and interaction for the benefit of the learner. Learner-centered design and delivery has never been more important than it is in every aspect of distance learning. Unlike commercial television, successful distance learning requires that the instructor do less and the learner do more.

Teaching networks must adopt what is best from the world of television— for example, production techniques that make television engaging and motivating—while rejecting entirely the instructor-centered studio bias upon which it is based, a practice that completely neglects the learner.

Not the Traditional Classroom

Is distance learning simply a glorified and extended traditional classroom? Definitely not. A traditional delivery that is repeated verbatim in front of a camera is doomed to fail. Distance learning requires three things not always found in traditional classroom teaching: learner-centered design, learner-centered delivery skills, and direct learner participation.

Today's classes, whether on university campuses, in public school classrooms, or in corporate training centers, are far more instructor centered than distance learning demands. Instructor-centered design results from the common practice of planning only what the instructor will do. We painstakingly identify instructional objectives, then develop a content outline from which we create presentations that are invariably delivered exclusively by the instructor. Little or no attention is paid to what we expect the learners to be doing.

We do not achieve similar learner involvement in our classes, because we typically set no objectives in that regard. Every lesson plan for a distance learning class should include specific and measurable involvement objectives to assure optimum levels of learner participation. We must design everything learners will do to the same extent that we now plan the duties of the instructor.

Once an ideal model for distance learning has been envisioned, it is time to take a look at the specific technologies and tools that make it possible. Why is this important? Because an instructor will be able to maximize the involvement of each learner only after understanding and mastering the system. Instructors who are uninformed and unskillful in execution cannot perform well for the benefit of the learners.

A Choice of Technologies

Two differing technologies deliver live video, with very different results. They are referred to in common usage by the types of images they can deliver: one-way video and two-way video.

One-way video is the name given the technology used to bring commercial television entertainment to the home; in teaching networks, one-way video is usually delivered by satellite or microwave systems. The instructor's video image originates from one location and is broadcast to all other sites, going only one way. The instructor in the studio can be seen by all others but cannot see the learners. Oral interaction takes place by telephone, using a telephone link that is established separately. Students are faceless to the instructor, but they do have voices. Adapting to this "faceless" environment is the most difficult adjustment for traditional classroom instructors, who are accustomed to seeing their students, reading body language, and so on.

Two-way video systems allow all sites and all participants to see and be seen, to hear and be heard, all through one system. Since the instructor can see the students and students can see the instructor, the system is dubbed "two-way video." As most two-way video systems have only one or two display screens at each location, incoming images must be viewed in sequence, not all at the same time. In other words, even though the instructor can hear all the students all of the time, students are seen by turns. Most systems rely on voice activation; that is, the person who is speaking becomes the image seen by all others.

One other distinction should be noted. Although it is technically possible to link up many locations with two-way video technology, in common practice such systems are used for smaller numbers of participating locations. One-way video classes delivered by satellite routinely link tens or hundreds of sites and hundreds or thousands of students, but two-way video classes typically connect fewer than ten locations. Thus, the total number of students in two-way video classes more closely replicates the average attendance in a traditional classroom. This fact should not be construed as either a limitation or a benefit, as learning can occur with either type of system as long as the design and delivery are appropriate for the medium.

Any instructor who is scheduled to teach in a video classroom should first ascertain which type of system will be used and how many sites and learners will be directly involved.

A Choice of Environments

The new video instructor may encounter two greatly different teaching environments: a video studio or an instructional classroom. These environments differ not only in how they are equipped and staffed but in what is expected of the instructors who teach in them.

The studio. Organizations with a long history of television production often originate their programs from a regular television studio. Instructors are expected to teach from a lighted video set surrounded by one to four cameras and supported by a number of crew members. Clearly, this environment represents the greatest change and challenge to the traditional instructor.

The instructional classroom. High overhead and staffing costs associated with full studio production have forced many teaching networks to seek a less costly solution. In the 1980s, experiments by user organizations and technology improvements by vendors resulted in the development of the instructional classroom, which has now been widely adopted. Unlike a studio, the instructional classroom has many automated functions and often includes robotic cameras and touch-screen controls. The instructor, perhaps assisted by one aide, operates all video tools and selects and transmits the appropriate image at the appropriate time. Other elements of video production—such as customized lighting and sets and extensive crew support—have vanished. Instructors in these settings teach from what is basically an enhanced classroom rather than from a television studio.

The Instructor's Role

The most crucial difference in the instructor's role when teaching from a video studio is the loss of autonomy. In the traditional classroom, the instructor delivers all the presentations, displays all the visuals, runs all the equipment, and is basically in charge. In the studio environment, the instructor is but one member of a larger team.

In the video studio a number of crew members are engaged to handle many of the chores traditionally done by the instructor. Instead of working alone, the instructor must coordinate every action with a number of other people. A written outline of what will occur (the rundown sheet) must be developed, followed by extensive rehearsal with the crew to assure a smooth delivery of every aspect of the class. Instead of making all decisions in a vacuum, the instructor must now defer to a director, who has ultimate responsibility for the course delivery. This transition from solo performer to team player can be a difficult one for the traditionally trained instructor.

In the instructional classroom, the dilemma facing the instructor is that of too little support, not too much. Instead of being surrounded by familiar chalkboards, flip charts, or overhead projectors, the instructor encounters an array of classroom oddities, which can include a touch-screen control panel, an annotation pen, a computer mouse or keyboard, a document camera, and the like. No team of crew members awaits to fulfill the instructor's every command. Instead, all video tools are to be operated by one person—the instructor. Teaching while operating these devices can seem as unnatural as rubbing one's stomach and patting one's head simultaneously.

Mastering the Equipment

The only way to become comfortable with all of this technology is to practice until every tool is an old friend and its operation becomes second nature. Extensive practice should be mandatory for all primary instructors, not just for those in the instructional classroom. Those who will teach from a studio may need to use a TelePrompTer or earpiece microphone for the first time; certainly eye contact with the cameras will need to be practiced.

How much practice is recommended? If you have to stop and think about where to look or which button to push, you haven't practiced long enough. One successful Michigan network requires eight hours of practice for every hour of instruction, before new instructors are allowed to teach at a distance.

Preparing the Instructor's Area

One way to assure the highest degree of comfort in either teaching environment is to make it your own. Instructors are not robots; they teach in different ways, using a variety of teaching styles. Whether you teach from a video studio or an instructional classroom, take the time to look over the teaching area and to make some adjustments that better suit you and your teaching style.

Decide whether you will stand or sit, and arrange the chairs and other furnishings accordingly. Move the document camera to a slight angle; doing so usually results in a more comfortable and natural handwriting position. If you tend to wander around when you teach, use masking tape to mark the outer limits of movement; the tape will indicate how far you can move and still be in the camera shot when standing in your primary teaching position. If you must operate the cameras yourself, create one or two optimum shots of yourself based on your height and store them as pre-sets that can be recalled quickly without a lot of panning and zooming.

Besides adjusting the equipment, consider the nonelectronic essentials. Mentally walk through your upcoming lesson and check to be sure you have all other materials—papers, textbooks, pens, objects to display or demonstrate, and the like—close at hand and ready for the lesson you have designed.

Too many instructors walk into the studio or instructional classroom at the last minute and just begin teaching. No teaching area has yet been designed to accommodate every single instructor without some slight personal modifications. Good preparation is reflected in a well-delivered class; you owe it to the learners to teach from a comfortable and efficient environment.

Understanding the Learner's Environment

Make a special effort to understand the learning environment of your students as well. Which time zones and cities will be included? Will learners congregate in small or large groups? Will there be a large number of locations for your course or just a few? Will they all be similarly equipped? Does any part of your lesson indicate the need for additional on-site support, such as a site facilitator?

Such learner demographics are important during the course design phase, but they are also critically important for the actual delivery. If you are to direct activities and interaction skillfully, you first need to know how many students you have and where they all are. Whenever possible, prepare a written list of students who are expected to attend, grouped by their location. Take it to class and use it to track oral participation by site or by individual. If preregistration is not possible, or if it results in an inaccurate or incomplete attendance tally, have students prepare site lists and fax them as an opening activity.

Skillful Facilitation

After technical arrangements have been made, the lesson has been designed, and students are in attendance, the success of the subsequent lesson depends upon the facilitation skill of the instructor. Every teacher must establish an open, inviting, and nonthreatening learning environment. If, on the other hand, student comments are treated as an interruption or a nuisance, a high degree of interactivity and involvement will not be achieved, regardless of the lesson plan.

Don't wait for students to ask you questions, but use directed questions to include and involve all sites and all learners. Just as you wouldn't rely solely on student-initiated questions in the traditional classroom, neither should you in distance learning. Call on sites and individuals to assure that students are paying attention and understanding the lesson.

If you expect students to talk to you, you must support their efforts. Questions that can have a wrong or right answer are better asked of a site than of an individual. Everyone at that location can contribute to the answer, which is determined by consensus. When students volunteer a comment or a question, thank them for their contributions and build on their ideas as a form of acknowledgment. If they ask you a question, follow up personally to be sure that they understood the answer before moving on to another student or topic.

Often how we say something is just as important as what we say. Facilitation skills can be greatly improved by carefully selecting the terms and phrases used to invite students to participate. Saying, "Are there any questions?" is one of the worst ways to stimulate discussion. That particular phrase does not specify a particular person or location, and the learners cannot tell from the monitor to whom you are directing the question, so they have no idea who is supposed to speak. The request for questions only deters those who might want to contribute something other than a question, such as a comment, a different opinion, an idea, or an example. It is far better to kick off discussion by calling on a particular person or a particular site and asking for ideas, comments, or questions. You will get what you ask for, so think a bit before you speak, and choose your words carefully.

Finally, skillful facilitation means that students always understand what is expected of them. Instructions for learning activities should be concise and to the point and should be accompanied by written instructions on the television screen and in handouts, if possible.

Skillful facilitation is the culmination of your efforts. Improve your facilitation skills by videotaping classes and critiquing your own delivery.

Final Thoughts

Experienced instructors who are successful in front of a video camera will be at the forefront of education, as the trend to the delivery of live video classes to geographically distant learners is not likely to abate. Success in this medium results from understanding the medium and the instructor's environment and then mastering the equipment and acquiring facilitation skills that allow the instructor to motivate and directly involve all learners. Distance learning offers new challenges to established instructors that can result in untold benefits to remote learners and a greater degree of personal satisfaction with teaching.

Reference

Ostendorf, V. A. *Distance Learning Directory*. (5th ed.) Littleton, Colo.: Virginia A. Ostendorf, 1996.

VIRGINIA A. OSTENDORF *is president of Virginia A. Ostendorf, Inc. and the founder of the Ostendorf Center for Distance Learning in Littleton, Colorado.*

Teaching by telephone may be one of the original distance education media, but it still has an important place in the array of media available for distance learning.

Teaching by Telephone

Christine H. Olgren

The telephone has a long and rich history as a distance learning technology that is often overshadowed by the more enticing media of video, computers, and multimedia. For nearly half a century, however, the telephone has proven to be an effective tool for providing education and training to students throughout the world.

This chapter describes key considerations in teaching by telephone, including (1) knowing the medium's strengths and limitations, (2) designing for the audio medium, (3) using teaching and humanizing methods that foster cognitive and affective engagement, and (4) managing the on-line audio environment.

Background on Telephone Teaching

Although early applications of telephone teaching go back to the 1930s and 1940s, the large-scale use of the telephone for distance education took root in the 1960s and grew rapidly in the 1970s and 1980s (Olgren and Parker, 1983). By 1986 at least seventy colleges and universities in the United States were using audio teleconferencing to provide college credit and continuing education programs to distance learners (Olgren, 1986).

The University of Wisconsin Extension, for example, established a telephone network in 1965 to serve nearly two hundred communities across the state with continuing education programs, mainly for physicians. Today, the Extension's Educational Teleconferencing Network (ETN) is used by more than fifty UW departments to reach thousands of participants annually with a variety of university credit and noncredit programs. The university now employs various distance learning systems, including compressed video, satellite video, computer conferencing, and World Wide Web, but teaching by telephone continues to be an important option in providing wide access to UW teaching resources.

NEW DIRECTIONS FOR TEACHING AND LEARNING, no. 71, Fall 1997 © Jossey-Bass Publishers

In a quarter-century of telephone teaching, the University of Wisconsin Extension has found that 80 to 85 percent of all participants are comfortable with audio and would recommend audio courses to others (Baird, 1989). Scores of other studies have found that students learn as much in telephone teaching as they do in video or face-to-face instruction (Fowler and Wackerbarth, 1980; Clark, 1983; Garrison, 1990; Russell, 1992; Moore and Thompson, 1990).

Technology

To provide education and training programs, telephone teaching typically employs some type of audio teleconferencing system. Audio teleconferencing is defined as the use of voice-only telephone technology to link multiple sites that are distant from one another. The number of sites on-line for a program can range from a few to several hundred, but twenty to thirty is average. The sites may comprise individuals in their homes or offices and/or groups gathered at learning centers or in rooms equipped with speakerphone systems.

Compared to other distance education media, audio technology is relatively simple. It basically requires access to a telephone or speakerphone and a way to link multiple locations. Linking can be accomplished by a conference call, a teleconference bridge, or a private-line telephone network. Because audio quality is important, equipment designed for teleconferencing, along with technical support, are recommended.

Strengths and Limitations

The key to effective telephone teaching is to capitalize on its strengths and compensate for its limitations. That is, the instructor should use course designs and teaching methods that are adapted to the medium. As Kozma (1994) emphasized, a medium's capabilities are important considerations in supporting the cognitive, affective, and social processes of learning.

The two audio technology capabilities that most affect course design and teaching methods are its strength in being an interactive medium and its limitation in lacking visual cues. To capitalize on audio's strength for two-way verbal communication, the instructor should employ interactive teaching methods that engage students in active learning through discussion, question-and-answer, problem solving, and other activities that support mental processes. To compensate for audio's lack of nonverbal cues, the instructor should use humanizing techniques to create a supportive climate for affective and social learning as well as supplementary print materials.

Exhibit 8.1 summarizes the strengths and limitations of audio teleconferencing as an instructional medium, drawing on practical experience and research (Ostendorf, 1989; Monson, 1977; Fowler and Wackerbarth, 1980; Wellens, 1986; Burge and Howard, 1990; Garrison, 1990).

Exhibit 8.1. Strengths and Limitations of Audio Technology

Strengths

Two-way verbal communication. Audio systems are interactive and enable all participants to talk to one another in a natural discussion format.

Accessibility. Telephones are widely available and readily accessible.

Flexibility. Instructors and students can participate from anywhere there is a telephone.

Cost. Audio is the least expensive electronic technology for distance learning, compared to video, audiographics, computer conferencing, and multimedia.

Ease of use. Audio systems are relatively easy to use compared to other electronic technologies.

Support for a variety of instructional activities. Audio is effective for many types of instructional or communication activities, including presenting ideas, exchanging information, discussion, problem solving, brainstorming, interviewing, and decision making.

Limitations

Voice-only communication. Participants cannot see each other, and visual information must be provided through supplementary print, graphics, photographs, slides, videotapes, computer disks, or World Wide Web pages.

Increased interpersonal distance. The lack of nonverbal cues can contribute to feelings of greater psychological distance, making it harder to get to know someone, create group rapport, negotiate, or resolve conflicts.

A more formal climate. The lack of nonverbal cues can create a more formal, businesslike atmosphere.

More tiring. Because audio requires concentrated listening, it is more tiring than face-to-face or video instruction.

Guidelines for Effective Telephone Teaching

Effective telephone teaching does not occur by accident; it is a product of careful planning and design decisions. Presented below, in a simplified outline form, are guidelines covering the major elements involved in designing a program for telephone teaching. The guidelines draw on the pioneering work done at the University of Wisconsin Extension (Monson, 1977, 1978; Baird, 1977), as well as my own experience in telephone teaching.

A. Before the program
   1. Plan ahead. Audio teleconferences should be well planned and organized, with a clear picture of how the program will accomplish objectives. Like other media, audio tends to magnify poor planning.
   2. Put together a print package. Include an outline or syllabus, participation instructions, participant roster, instructor biography and photo, readings, evaluation form, a list of who to call for help, and other

materials to prepare students for learning and the audio experience. Use an interactive study guide (Cyrs and Smith, 1991), if appropriate.

3. Design for the audio medium.

Plan for a sixty-minute to two-hour format. Include one or more short breaks. Because audio is more tiring than video or face-to-face instruction, listener concentration fades after two hours, even with a midpoint break. Some instructors, however, use a three-hour format with good results.

Cover only three to five concepts per hour. Elaborate on main ideas with explanations, examples, stories, and real-life experiences relevant to the learners. Summarize after each concept.

Design for short segments of five, ten, or fifteen minutes. Use a variety of instructional activities, such as fifteen minutes of presentation followed by ten minutes of discussion and five minutes of brainstorming.

Incorporate visuals, such as graphics, to aid understanding or application of main ideas. Stimulate visual thinking about abstract concepts by using verbal descriptions that invite mental images or familiar examples, scenes, or analogies.

4. Add variety to presentation methods. For a change of pace from short lectures, use guest speakers, tandem teaching, peer teaching, or interviews to present information.

5. Plan interactive teaching activities. Engage learners in interacting with the instructor, the content, and other students. As a general guideline, at least 30 percent of a one-hour block should be devoted to interactive activities. Examples are question-and-answer sessions, discussion, problem solving, brainstorming, case studies, debates, reactor panels, role playing, small-group subconferences, and group work at the local sites. These activities work best when participants feel comfortable with the technology and with sharing ideas. Before an activity, the instructor should prepare participants by creating a supporting and encouraging climate, clarifying what is expected, and starting with easier activities (such as question and answer or discussion) to help learners get warmed up or gain confidence. Include activity descriptions in the program's print package. During the activity, the instructor's role is typically to guide interaction by acting as a moderator or facilitator.

6. Plan for humanizing techniques. Acknowledge individuals and create group rapport to compensate for audio's tendency to be impersonal and formal. Examples are sending a welcome letter, calling participants by name, asking participants about their backgrounds, jotting down and referring to individuals' interests, recalling someone's previous comments, and speaking conversationally.

7. Develop an agenda or instructional plan. For each audio session, prepare an agenda that guides the instructor in the timing, sequencing, and handling of each topic and activity. Include as much detail and

scripting as needed to feel organized and confident, but be prepared to modify the agenda during the program in response to learning needs and conditions. The three most common mistakes in planning for telephone teaching are too much content, too little time per topic or activity, and too little interaction.

8. Be familiar with the technology. Know how to use the microphone system and what to do if technical problems arise. Practice before the program.

B. During the program

1. Establish a friendly atmosphere. At the start of a program, set a climate of warmth and participation by welcoming participants, conversing informally for a few minutes, and using people's names. Take an informal roll call, interspersed with occasional questions about local sites. Informal conversations also help learners to become comfortable using the technology.

2. Provide a short overview. State briefly the program's general theme or main ideas. Draw attention to pertinent print or visual materials. Review briefly the previous session (if there was one).

3. Explain telephone etiquette. List the teleconferencing ground rules so students know the correct behavior. Ask people to (1) say their names before making a comment or asking a question ("This is Jill Jones, and I have a question about . . ."); (2) speak directly into their speakerphones so that they can be heard clearly; (3) use the mute button on their speakerphones during listening segments to reduce background noise; and (4) report when it is difficult to hear someone. Avoid asking repeatedly whether people can hear you.

4. Present information clearly. Clarity is essential if verbal messages are to be received and understood. Vary vocal pitch and pacing to make listening more enjoyable.

5. Manage the audio environment. In addition to managing content and teaching-learning activities, the instructor must manage four key elements in the audio environment: sound quality, time, climate, and participation. Ongoing monitoring and adjusting of these factors in the absence of nonverbal cues involves both techniques and art gained through practice. Here are some tips to get started.

   Sound quality. Be alert for audio problems, such as background noise, weak voices, or static on the line. If problems occur, remind participants of etiquette ground rules, or ask a site to hang up and redial to obtain a better connection. When problems are not readily solved, contact the technician or troubleshooting number.

   Time. Start and end on time. Use an agenda to help monitor time, but make adjustments as needed. Employ summaries or transitions to let people know it is time to change topics.

   Climate. Maintain a friendly climate and group rapport by using humanizing techniques as described earlier. Have an annotated class roster on hand for ready reference to participants' names and backgrounds.

Participation. When asking learners to respond to questions, give them time to compose their answers by waiting up to ten seconds. Explain the ten-second guideline so that people feel comfortable with silences (ten seconds can seem like a long time in audio). Monitor participation levels and respond to underparticipation or overparticipation. Simple techniques for responding to underparticipation include directing questions to people or sites ("Joe, what do you think?" "Does someone in Eau Claire want to add to that?"), asking questions that draw on participants' backgrounds ("Mary, can you give us an example from your experience?"), establishing a round-robin discussion format, or assigning study questions in advance. To respond to overparticipation by an individual or site, ask for other opinions ("Let's get some other people's ideas on this") or direct questions to other sites. A round-robin format of taking turns can also help control for individual overparticipation.

6. Provide and ask for feedback. Because more verbal feedback is needed to compensate for the absence of visual cues, listen carefully to students' responses and correct misunderstandings. Ask for feedback from students about the clarity of your own messages. Evaluate the program at midpoint to make improvements and at the end to assess effectiveness.

7. Provide a wrap-up at the end of the program. Summarize main ideas, thank people for participating, and provide an overview of the next session (in a multisession course).

C. After the program
1. Review program evaluation results. Listen to audiotapes of the program. Use the results to improve future programs and vocal delivery.

Other Considerations

Like any instructional program, planning for an audio course should include a front-end analysis of learning needs and content requirements in order to develop appropriate learning objectives and teaching strategies. Additional factors are involved when planning a total telephone teaching system. Those factors include faculty training and incentives, availability of audio-visual services, technical support for maintenance and troubleshooting, course scheduling, marketing, and student registration procedures. Distance learners may require support services, such as access to advising or library resources. If an audio system is to serve groups of learners clustered at distant sites, then decisions are needed about site location, room environment, and local coordination.

Finally, audio teleconferencing is not just a delivery system to transmit information across distances. It is a teaching-learning environment that should engage students in knowledge development through interactive activities that stimulate critical thinking, integration with prior learning, and testing in real-world applications. As Anderson and Garrison (1995) found, designing for interaction and critical discourse has a profound impact on students' perceptions of the quality and value of their learning. Such engagement in learning is engendered not only by interactive teaching methods but also by humanizing techniques that help to build a community of inquiry through interpersonal relationships and group rapport.

References

Anderson, T. D., and Garrison, R. D. "Transactional Issues in Distance Education: The Impact of Design in Audioteleconferencing." *American Journal of Distance Education,* 1995, *9* (2), 27–45.

Baird, M. "Designing Teleconferencing Programs: Some Clues from the Wisconsin Experience." In M. Monson, L. Parker, and B. Riccomini (eds.), *A Design for Interactive Audio.* Madison: Instructional Communications Systems, University of Wisconsin Extension, 1977.

Baird, M. "Wisconsin Teleconferencing Service Marks 24th Year of Outreach and Growth." In *UITCA Teleconferencing Yearbook.* Washington, D.C.: International Teleconferencing Association, 1989.

Burge, E. J., and Howard, J. L. "Audio-Conferencing in Graduate Education: A Case Study." *American Journal of Distance Education,* 1990, 4 (2), 3–13.

Clark, R. E. "Reconsidering Research on Learning from Media." *Review of Educational Research,* 1983, 53 (4), 445–459.

Cyrs, T. E., and Smith, F. A. "Designing Interactive Study Guides with Word Pictures for Teleclass Teaching." *TechTrends,* 1991, 36 (1), 37–39.

Fowler, G. D., and Wackerbarth, M. E. "Audio Teleconferencing Versus Face-to-Face Conferencing: A Synthesis of the Literature." *Western Journal of Speech Communication,* 1980, 44, 236–252.

Garrison, D. R. "An Analysis and Evaluation of Audio Teleconferencing to Facilitate Education at a Distance." *American Journal of Distance Education,* 1990, 4 (3), 13–24.

Kozma, R. B. "Will Media Influence Learning? Reframing the Debate." *Educational Technology Research and Development,* 1994, 442 (2),7–19.

Monson, M. "A Report Investigating Teaching Techniques Used over the Educational Telephone Network." In M. Monson, L. Parker, and B. Riccomini (eds.), *A Design for Interactive Audio.* Madison: Instructional Communications Systems, University of Wisconsin Extension, 1977.

Monson, M. *Bridging the Distance: An Instructional Guide to Teleconferencing.* Madison: Instructional Communications Systems, University of Wisconsin Extension, 1978.

Moore, M. G., and Thompson, M. M. *The Effects of Distance Learning: A Review of the Literature.* Research monograph no. 2. University Park: American Center for the Study of Distance Education, Pennsylvania State University, 1990.

Olgren, C. H. *The CIP Teleconferencing Directory.* (9th ed.) Madison: Center for Interactive Programs, University of Wisconsin Extension, 1986.

Olgren, C. H., and Parker, L. A. *Teleconferencing Technology and Applications.* Dedham, Mass.: Artech House, 1983.

Ostendorf, V. A. *What Every Principal, Teacher, and School Board Member Should Know About Distance Education.* Littleton, Colo.: Virginia A. Ostendorf, 1989.

Russell, T. "The 'No Significant Difference' Phenomenon as Reported in Reassert Reports, Summaries, and Papers." Unpublished manuscript. Raleigh: North Carolina State University, 1992.

Wellens, A. R. "Use of a Psychological Distancing Model to Assess Differences in Telecommunication Media." In L. A. Parker and C. H. Olgren (eds.), *Teleconferencing and Electronic Communications V*. Madison: Center for Interactive Programs, University of Wisconsin Extension, 1986.

CHRISTINE H. OLGREN is distance education manager at the University of Wisconsin-Madison.

*An outline of the basic features of the Internet and World Wide Web
environment is presented, along with suggestions regarding how these
features can be used for creating on-line learning environments and
promoting wired learning activities.*

The Internet: A Learning Environment

Rory McGreal

Jennifer in San Diego is sitting in front of her monitor exchanging messages
with Bill in Springfield, Illinois. She has just received responses from her professor to several questions she posed early this morning. Bill and Jennifer are
working on an assignment together for their first-year nursing course at the
University of New Brunswick (UNB) in Canada: Identifying Instances of Child
Abuse. Neither student has even visited Canada.

Bill advises Jennifer to double-check the lecture notes from last week, which
are available at the UNB Web site. Jennifer is forwarding some relevant articles,
one from a medical database at the University of Washington and the others from
a Web site at the University of New South Wales. Bill is sending along to her the
comments from several experts with whom he has discussed their topic on-line.
They are preparing for a live on-line presentation of their research using Web
videoconferencing next week. This will be followed by an on-line test.

A far-fetched scenario? Not really. The tools and strategies included in this
vignette are available today. The purpose of this chapter is to introduce the
reader to the possibilities for distance education through the Internet and the
World Wide Web.

Some Background and Terminology

The Internet and the World Wide Web are becoming integrated into a common
environment that is suitable for many different types of learning activities. With
Web browsers like Netscape, Mosaic, and Microsoft Explorer, you can explore

---

This chapter is on-line in hypertext with links to the teacher's manual, *Learning on the Web*
[http://tenb.mta.ca].

on-line worlds of all types, ranging from virtual universities to weather stations, movie studies, companies, and personal sites with unique information.

The Internet is a distributed network in which there is no center. Large numbers of computers connected via a range of media hold textual, graphical, audio, and other materials that are available to anyone to access. No one controls this global web.

Anyone with a computer, a modem, and a telephone connection can get on-line and "surf." For teachers, this can be a major benefit, opening up new worlds of knowledge for students. On the other hand this very access can cause serious problems when students can easily access unsavory sites or come in contact on-line with people of questionable character.

Accessing the Internet for the first time has been known to cause migraines even in people with strong computer skills. Fortunately, in many regions local entrepreneurs are setting up as Internet service providers to supply people with the initial tools and advise them during that critical first connection. (An industry magazine publishes a directory of more than fourteen thousand Internet service providers in the United States and Canada [Boardwatch, n.d.].) Once connected, few special skills are required for most tasks, although a basic knowledge of computers, databases, and search strategies is highly recommended. Many tutorials are available on-line free of charge for learning Internet navigation and other skills.

The Internet is available to anyone, anywhere, at any time of the day or night. Because it is always accessible, people can stay in touch *asynchronously* (at different times). Messages can be posted at midnight and read the following day. Teachers can respond to students at their convenience, not having to keep specific office hours. The World Wide Web is a *hypermedia* environment on the Internet. Hypermedia allows users to hop from site to site simply by clicking on text or graphical "hot spots" (highlighted text, a button, or a graphic). For example, you might visit a museum Web site in Washington that has links to other museums around the world. Links can be made to text, a graphic, video, sound, or even three-dimensional virtual reality. The Web is now so popular that it is almost becoming the Internet as more features are accessible using a simple Web browser.

A Web browser is used to navigate around the Internet. You can use Web browsers like Netscape, Mosaic, and Microsoft Explorer to navigate or surf the Internet. They have become all-purpose tools not only for surfing but also for interacting, communicating, and searching. New tools called plug-ins and helpers combine with Web browsers to open up a whole new world of possibilities in publishing, animation, videoconferencing, virtual reality, and interactive simulation.

Another feature of the Internet is the anonymity that is possible. People do not see you and need not know anything about you. Many people take advantage of this feature to adopt alternative personalities and visit virtual worlds for on-line games and other interactions. Internet users need to be aware of this and should not simply assume that people are who they say they are.

Some popular searching tools, like Gopher, Archie, Veronica, and Wais, are disappearing or are being integrated into the World Wide Web. These have been the principal search tools until recently. Web-based services have replaced them. Alta Vista, Infoseek, Lycos, Magellan, WebCrawler, Yahoo, and others are all easily accessible through a Web browser.

In addition, the widely used protocols Telnet and FTP (File Transfer Protocol) can now be used directly through Web browsers, although many users prefer to use specific tools. Telnet can be used to get into remote computers to use software and to access information remotely. FTP is used to download files from (or upload files to) a remote computer.

There are thousands of newsgroups on the Internet. They are normally focused on a particular topic. People who are interested in that topic can click on the topic name and read the messages or post a message if they desire. Newsgroups can be accessed through a Web browser.

Sending and receiving e-mail is still the most popular activity on the Internet. Many use software like Eudora, Pegasus, Microsoft Exchange, or Pine. Others are using the mail features available in their Web browsers. Through e-mail, users can access mailing lists or listservs. Listservs consist of discussion groups on particular topics, often including many people who are experts in a particular field. They differ from newsgroups in that a user must sign up to join a particular listserv. (The difference between them is like the difference between having to pick up a magazine at the corner store and being a subscriber with home delivery.) Listserv messages are sent directly from the list to your personal mailbox. Computer-mediated conferencing (CMC) is the term used for on-line discussions using these tools or other more specialized software.

Sending and receiving messages *synchronously* (in real time) is possible using IRC (Internet Relay Chat). In IRC, participants type messages to each other or to a group, and the messages are read immediately; in CMC the messages are read later on. MUDs (Multi-User Dungeons) and MOOs (MUDs Object-Oriented) are virtual worlds in which you can interact electronically with other participants. These have been text-based but are increasingly being used within a visual environment. Some of these virtual worlds are three-dimensional, using VRML (Virtual Reality Modeling Language). Educational institutions are experimenting with them as Virtual Educational Environments (VEEs) or MUSHes (Multi-User Shared Hallucinations). These real-time conferences can be conducted over the Internet using audio and video connections. Such conferences are still a little primitive, especially at a lower bandwidth. Not many computers have the capacity for seamless two-way conversations, and only choppy video images are possible with most standard modems.

Back to Our Opening Scenario

In the example with which we started this chapter, Jennifer is using IRC to communicate directly with Bill. Her professor has left her several e-mail messages. She will check the lecture notes at her course Web site. The articles she accessed were FTPed from the University of Washington and downloaded directly from the Web site in Australia. Bill got into the UNB computer using his Telnet software, but Jennifer is more comfortable using her Web browser. She is using her e-mail to forward the articles as attachments. Bill is attaching the transcript of an on-line discussion he copied from a newsgroup. The presentation next week will be possible using CU-SeeMe on-line videoconferencing software. The test will be made available at the UNB Web site as an on-line form.

Using Internet Technology for Instruction

Different styles of learning are possible using the Internet. Lectures, seminars, forums, on-line tutorials, expert consultations, and other class models are all possible. But whatever the model chosen, every Web-based course should include the following basic pages:

Home page. This is the first page that students will see. It should be kept short, containing only the most essential information about the course or program, including the title, the name of the organization, and your geographical location (town, state or province, and country). There should be no scrolling; all information should fit on a standard screen. Avoid the temptation to include a large graphic that takes ages to appear.

Introduction. Write a short description of the course or program, with links to descriptions about your organization. Also include the following: a greeting, a list of credits naming everyone who has worked on the project, a date of last update notice, an e-mail link to a contact person, and a hyperlink to the full course syllabus, if it is available.

Course overview (road map). Provide an overview of the structure of the course or program, including a brief description of each module or section, along with a table of contents. The goals and objectives of the course must be clearly stated.

Course requirements. List all required course materials, including texts, courseware, manuals, significant on-line resources, links, and other tools and media materials, such as computer equipment and software tools. This should include the minimum computer configuration and links for downloading the Web browser and required plug-ins.

Vital information. Include direct e-mail links to the teacher and tutors; their surface mail addresses; their voice and fax telephone numbers; their on-line office hours; links to other services like registration, admissions, transcripts, guidance, library, and so on; and a link to pages outlining institutional policies.

Roles and responsibilities. You can never make the respective roles and responsibilities of the teacher, tutors, and students too clear. Students should have an outline of what is expected of them in the course, including how they will be graded and all assignment deadlines.

Assignments. Include a list of all the assignments or tasks required of students, along with their due dates, and links to other activities for remedial or advanced work.

Course schedule. Provide a calendar outlining the significant events of the course, for example, assignment due dates, quizzes, examinations, special electronic visits, and outside activities. Even in self-paced courses, a sample schedule will help students to pace themselves. A final deadline for course completion would also be helpful in motivating procrastinators to complete their assignments.

Resources. Include a page with links to outside resources that are relevant to the course or program.

Sample tests. Provide a page that lists examples of test questions or links to examples of successfully completed assignments.

Biography. Include short biographies of the teacher, tutor, and others, including their photos and links to curriculum vitae and other details, if appropriate.

Course or program evaluation. Offer a questionnaire for students to use to evaluate the course.

Glossary and index. This page should contain a glossary of the new terms used in the course or program. If possible, include an index with a full-text search facility for quick navigation.

Conferencing area. This is an area where students and teacher can meet on-line for text discussions. These conferences can be conducted asynchronously, where the students and teachers post messages at their convenience, or synchronously, where the class meets together for real-time text-based discussions.

Bulletin board. Provide a page or pages where students and teachers can post announcements. Some can be specific to a course; others can be left open to encourage general announcements.

FAQ pages. These pages answer frequently asked questions about the course, program, institution, and other relevant sectors.

How to learn. Programs should be accompanied by modules on how to learn in an on-line environment.

Although there are no clear answers, before embarking on a Web project, the questions in Exhibit 9.1 should be thought through based on your particular situation. These questions cover only some of the ground that needs to be considered. Still, they should give you an idea of the issues and the complexity of a Web course project.

Suggestions for Designing a Course Web Site

Do:

Use examples and interesting content from other Web sites.
Archive the classroom discussion groups and make them accessible to future students.
Put all your lecture notes and other important documents on-line.
Encourage students to make their own Web pages.
Encourage students to submit journals and create publications on-line.

Exhibit 9.1. Questions About Web-Based Teaching

1. Which computer system are you using for the server? For development? For the students?

Cheap	*Hardware*				Expensive
286 PC	386 PC	486 PC	Pentium	Sun workstation	UNIX box
Apple Macintosh			Power Mac		

2. What kind of software will you be using for the server? For development? For the students?

Cheap	*Software*				Expensive
Freeware	Shareware	Bundles	Off-the-shelf	Self-developed	Major project

3. What degree of security is required? Who can access how much? What controls are needed?

Open	*Security*				Closed
Listed	Unlisted	Password	Firewall		Closed network

4. How innovative do you want to be?

Cautious	*Innovation*				Leading Edge
E-mail Listservs	Gopher FTP Telnet	IRC MOOs	Audio Video	Real time	Virtual reality
Newsgroups			Web conferencing		

5. How much do you wish to control the development? Can you compromise?

Full	*Control of Development*				None
Individual	Cooperative	Open	Teams	Contracting out	Specialists

6. How much can you spend?

Low	*Cost of Courses*				High
Self-paced	Tutors	Large lectures	Small classes		Individual counseling

7. How much control will you allow the students?

Full	*Student Control*				Minimal
Self-paced	Tutorials	Deadlines	Scheduled labs		Class sessions

8. How much time do you have before the course starts?

Short	*Preparation Time*				Long
Teleconference	Computer conference	Correspondence course	Courseware		Multimedia video

Make templates for yourself and others to ensure consistency and save work.
Use some interactive programs, animations, video, and sound clips, but ensure
that they are appropriate and relevant to the lesson.
Encourage students to read relevant newsgroups and join appropriate listservs.
Use hyperlinks to "subject trails" to direct students on guided Web tours.
Point students to useful sites for on-line research.
Integrate off-line materials into the course (print journals, textbooks, and appa-
ratus).
Use FAQs (files of frequently asked questions), and update them regularly.

Avoid:

Overwhelming students with too much information. Limit information to one
idea per page. Use space freely.
Scrolling large bodies of text. Break up your text into short chunks of no more
than one or two screens.
Using too many video and sound clips. They take a long time to download, and
they can easily distract students and detract from the focus of the lesson.
Giving technical and mechanical information within the content sections. Use
hyperlinks.
"Click here" statements. Remember, not everyone has a mouse.
Using plain text without taking advantage of hypertext capabilities. Take advantage of the medium, but don't overdo it. A rule of thumb is to use no
more than three links per page.
Making essential hypertext links to outside servers. They could change. Ask to
mirror (copy) sites that you feel are essential for the course.
Using large, megabit images, especially in your home page. They take too long
to load and can be frustrating.

Checklist for Web Sites

- All the links are working and have been checked recently.
- Grammar and spelling have been verified.
- The content has not been altered.
- The site has been examined using different browsers.
- The course content is current and relevant.
- The institutional and course information is current.

You should also be aware of other issues. For example, many disabled
people use different kinds of interfaces that have difficulties interpreting graphics. Therefore, text-only alternatives should always be provided. Copyright
remains in force on-line, but many issues are waiting to be resolved. Offensive
materials on-line can cause problems for supervisors. Children can meet electronically with strangers.

Still, the World Wide Web opens up a whole new world for learning.
Teachers entering this world are faced with few models of good practice and

little guidance. Do you use it to supplement your classroom activities? Can you integrate Web-based material into your regular program? Can you go totally on-line? How flexible can you be? What kind of support can you provide students at a distance? These questions and others are open. Because the Web is constantly evolving, perhaps there will never be clear answers. But, boy, is it fun! Use it and enjoy it.

Reference

Boardwatch magazine. *Internet Service Providers.* Published bimonthly [http://www.board-watch.com].

RORY MCGREAL is the director of TeleEducation New Brunswick and a member of the executive board of the Canadian TeleLearning Research Network. E-mail: rmcgreal @unb.ca.

Recent advances in technology foreshadow a day when distance education will connect a student to a network of resources.

Networked Learning Environments

Alan G. Chute, Pamela K. Sayers, Richard P. Gardner

Our vision for distance learning is a seamless networked learning environment that integrates voice, video, and data connections among learners, instructors, experts, virtual libraries, the Internet, and support services. At the center is the distance learner, connected with both real-time and non-real-time links to these resources (Figure 10.1). Networked learning environments can make education and training more accessible, convenient, focused, effective, and cost-efficient for the learners and providers alike.

Distance learning networks make training and advanced education possible in cases where time and budgetary constraints make it difficult to organize face-to-face training. However, to make distance learning work, instructors and providers must harness the potential of synchronous and asynchronous communication technologies to create powerful, learner-centered networks.

Figure 10.1. The Networked Learning Environment

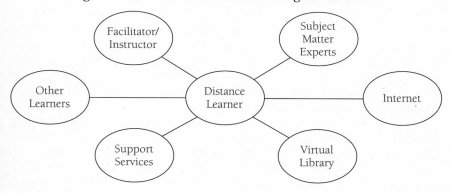

Synchronous communication technologies, such as desktop video teleconferencing and interactive group video teleconferencing, enable live, real-time interaction between instructors and learners. Instructors, subject matter experts, and learners see and hear one another at all sites and engage in interaction similar to face-to-face classroom interactions. *Asynchronous communication technologies,* such as e-mail, multimedia databases, virtual libraries, and the Internet, support non-real-time interactions and access to vast information resources at a time and place convenient to the learners.

The challenge is to implement the right combination of synchronous and asynchronous technologies to create a rich mosaic of networked learning environments consistent with the mission of the educational provider, learner expectations, and the delivery style of the instructor. For example, a desktop video teleconferencing network can link instructor and learners for presentation and discussion of key course concepts. The data collaboration capabilities of such a system enable the instructor and the learners to share software for simultaneously editing documents, completing spreadsheet exercises, or creating graphic presentations. Learners can continue the discussion through an e-mail network with other learners and subject matter experts. Additional multimedia resources like reference articles, journals, magazines, and video news clips can be accessed from a virtual library or the Internet to supplement and enrich the course content.

Distance learning networks can be used for all forms of education to improve the reach of programs, stretch education and training dollars, and deliver just-in-time educational content to learners anywhere, anytime.

The Need for Continuous Learning

During the latter part of the twentieth century, the need for continuous learning has changed and continues to change dramatically. The changing nature of work, from manufacturing to service, from pencil and paper to computer, points to the intense need for ongoing training and education.

The shape of the workforce is changing as well. From workers who change careers to new groups joining the workforce, job skill levels are changing just when the job skills required for success are becoming more varied and more advanced.

As we approach the beginning of the twenty-first century, there is a great need not only for more training and education but also for more effective and more efficient training. A key to success is the application of cost-effective technologies that distribute education and training electronically.

America's colleges and universities are also facing many challenges today. They need to prepare their learners for the emerging jobs in the information society. At the same time, they face shrinking institutional budgets. Traditional universities must develop new ways to reach nontraditional learner populations, who may not be on the campus or even in the same country. Networked learning environments make this possible.

Distance Learning Networks

Synchronous telecommunications networks for distance learning are generally divided into audio, audiographic, and video networks. The networks can be designed to accommodate large groups of learners, small groups, or even individuals working on their desktop PCs.

Audio networks function like a conference call, with the instructor directing the presentation of content and question-and-answer sessions. Each site is generally equipped with speakerphones or telephone headsets. The *audiographic network* combines the audio network with a shared graphic component—generally PC based so that all sites simultaneously view a common graphic presentation. Audio and audiographic networks operate on a plain old telephone service (POTS) analog line with a bridge to connect multiple sites.

Video networks generally employ digital telecommunication circuits and are divided into narrowband and broadband systems. A typical narrowband group video distance learning network has an instructor site and three or more remote sites connected via switched digital services or Integrated Services Digital Network (ISDN) circuits through a narrowband multipoint control unit (MCU). At the instructor site is a group video system that transmits video and audio of the instructor and receives video and audio from the remote learner sites. In addition, the instructor can supplement the lesson with graphics, slides, videotapes, and computer data (charts, presentation graphics, multimedia programs, and so on) through a number of available peripheral devices.

The remote sites are also equipped with group video systems. These are generally situated in a conference room or a standard classroom. All of the remote sites receive video and audio from the instructor site; learners at each site can see and hear the instructor as well as any audiovisual material from the instructor's peripheral devices. At the same time, the remote systems transmit video and audio from the learners to the instructor. The instructor, by using the MCU's universal conference control, can automatically or manually select which sites are seen and transmitted to all the other learner sites. The MCU's "continuous presence" feature permits the instructor to select simultaneous viewing of up to four remote sites at one time.

Teaching and Learning on a Network

The instructor in this environment becomes an orchestrator of multimedia technologies. Much like a conductor of a symphony orchestra, the instructor calls up inputs from various media sources to enhance the presentation. To be effective, the instructor needs to think of multiple ways to engage the learners in the class. Two key dimensions of effective programs are interaction and visual design.

Interaction is the most powerful way to engage learners. The instructor needs to design opportunities for inter-site and intra-site interactions among learners, at a minimum of about every twenty minutes. Question-and-answer periods, brainstorming sessions, case discussions, and role-playing exercise are examples of strategies the instructor can use to stimulate interaction.

Learners at remote sites often express the need to visually focus on something in their environment. Learners in audio programs feel uncomfortable staring at a speakerphone, so they often request handout materials that support the instructor's key points. In a video teleconference, the instructor should frequently switch between live video of the instructor and visual support material such as computer graphics, document camera input, and videotaped vignettes. Visual annotation of a computer graphic is an effective way to keep a static graphic visually stimulating.

The Role of Support Services

The technology infrastructure represents only one dimension of networked learning environments. Equally important, if not more important, is the human infrastructure that provides support services to the learners. The support services organization has a role like the customer services operation in a business enterprise. It provides administrative directions, emphatic listening, moral support, and conflict resolution services. For example, many learners today are still not comfortable with computer technology and will require some type of coaching to build up their confidence. By providing comprehensive support services to the learners, the educational providers will increase the learners' personal comfort zone with the distance learning environment and allow the learners to concentrate more on the subject and less on the technology.

Learners expect the instructions they receive for course registration, course access, and evaluation to be accurate, efficient, and trouble free. If they have trouble accessing or using the network, they expect someone to be available to help them. The more time learners spend trying to access the network or struggling with problems in its use, the less time they will devote to the course content.

The course of study itself must be well designed, must describe expected learner outcomes, and must be supported by an instructional and support staff available to address learners' concerns. The support services staff should be in a position to feed learner comments back to the instructor or course designer. If complaints about the content or the instructor continue, the support services staff should be able to counsel the learners and provide input to a quality control group that evaluates overall program effectiveness.

The course evaluation system should be designed to provide testing results quickly. One of the greatest concerns the learner may have is how to deal with a failure. It is important for the support services staff to reassure the learner regarding the evaluation process and inform the instructor of areas where learners have expressed concern. The support services organization must ensure that learners do not become so frustrated with a single failure that they opt to give up the course entirely.

Using the Internet

More and more, the Internet is becoming the vehicle for providing reference materials and up-to-date information. The Internet is now the preferred method for e-mail communication between learners and instructors. Learners like the ability to get their questions answered at a time and place convenient to their needs. Invariably, when learners who use e-mail regularly are asked if they found an Internet-based course to be interactive, they respond that the Internet course provided them more access to their instructors and other learners than their face-to-face courses.

While the Internet can be the method for providing learners the information they need, at a place and at the time they need it, there are a variety of issues that instructors and educational providers need to consider when placing course information and reference materials on the Internet.

Internet access. Will learners need their own computer, modem, and phone line? Are the learners able to get access to the Internet? If they do not have the technology, who will provide it? Once learners have the appropriate technology, can they locate your Web site easily? A Web site should be primarily text based so that learners with slower modems can easily access the information, but it is important to incorporate meaningful graphics where appropriate to enhance the learning experience. Future broadband networks will substantially remove restrictions on the amount and types of multimedia resources that can be accessed quickly by the learners.

Content hosting. The type of content placed on the Web should be interactive and relevant to the learners. An entire course need not be hosted; some content is best delivered in another form. It is important to incorporate some multimedia technology into the learning experience because it will provide the learner with a variety of methods to learn information. Incorporating technology such as audio, video, graphics, and e-mail interaction will provide a simulating learning experience for the learner; however, multimedia should be an enhancement to the course design, not a distraction.

Testing. Educational providers will often need to validate the learning experience, and testing on the Internet is becoming a reality. Testing on the Internet can be accomplished using traditional methods such as true or false, multiple-choice, and essay questions. Instructors using a system like the Indiana University Bureau of Evaluative Studies and Testing (http://www.best.indiana.edu) can go on-line and create test questions that can be immediately available for the learners' use. Learners can take the test at their leisure. Because learners have the ability to collaborate with others, some instructors use on-line testing only for quizzes and not for exams. However, this collaboration can be a very positive learning activity. When two or more learners get together to take a quiz, they are actually collaborating in a manner that would not have taken place in the traditional method. By collaborating, learners can get other viewpoints regarding a particular subject, thus enhancing the study group's learning.

Virtual Library Resources

Just as the campus library today provides an expansive repository of indexed information for residential students, the virtual library of the future will provide seamlessly integrated voice, video, and data resources for the distance learner. The virtual library will allow instructors to incorporate multimedia artifacts into teaching and networked learning environments. In fact, educational providers need to allow learners to create their own custom virtual libraries by "bookmarking" Web sites or even pages.

As technologies develop, many new forms of information can be included in virtual libraries. This will challenge instructors in both creating and accessing virtual libraries and incorporating them as resources for learners. Instructors and educational providers alike need to begin thinking about and planning for the tools that they will need to create, maintain, and use these virtual libraries as powerful agents for creating virtual learning environments.

Virtual Learning Environments

The learning environments that learners experience can be characterized in four ways:

Scenario	Time of Event for All Learners	Location of Event for All Learners
1	Same time	Same place
2	Same time	Different place
3	Different time	Same place
4	Different time	Different place

Each of these environments not only presents its own set of delivery issues but also creates issues for preserving the session so that it can be delivered to others later or simply used as a reference. Recording these sessions or components of the sessions (including PC-based interactions and the associated software), storing them, and indexing them for later retrieval are all aspects of creating and maintaining virtual learning environments.

Scenario One depicts what can be seen as a typical face-to-face learning environment. "Same time, same place" means that the learners and the instructor are all located in the same place at the same time for all attendees. However, even in a face-to-face scenario, the instructor may want to use information that was recorded at an earlier time, demonstrate features of a software package, or include a real-time visit by a subject matter expert at another location. Students asked to present information to peers during a face-to-face session may choose to incorporate prerecorded sources or may choose to go live onto the Internet to net-based source documents. Presession assignments or readings may have been presented via e-mail, or supporting materials may exist only in an electronic database and may need to be accessed during the face-to-face session. It is currently a challenge to capture such sessions or portions of them for use as a reference or by those not able to attend at the scheduled time.

Scenario Two (same time, different place) describes what is typically called a teletraining or teleconferencing program. Learners and instructor are not all at the same location, even though the session runs for the same time period for all attendees. Generally, the geographic separation of learners is overcome by audio or video teleconferencing. This scenario has grown from basic audio teleconferencing/teletraining to include video and data conferencing. The signals carried over the telecommunications circuits can be captured and then replayed on similar equipment at a later time and different place by the learner.

Scenario Three (different time, same place) is essentially the same as Scenario Two, except that one or more learners at the same place join the session after it has ended. They still "attend" the session and need to interact with the content of the session and with the learners. They may even want to send their session notes to the other learners for review and comment, or they may be in a study group with other learners and need to share session resources to prepare for a future session.

Scenario Four suggests that the learner is going to access the information not only at a later time but also from another location. This scenario includes a variant on Scenario Three as well as other forms of training, such as computer-based training (CBT) and electronic performance support systems (EPSS). The Internet or an intranet may be used to deliver CBT, but in many cases, because of the multimedia nature of the CBT and bandwidth limitations of the network the learners access, this may not be practical. However, it may be practical to use the network as a distribution medium. If that is to be done, the courses have to be stored along with information that helps the user find the right course. It is often helpful if an instructor provides an example of some portion of the course so that the learner can choose whether to download the course. This demo segment may work just fine on the network but may require a viewer. The virtual library must take all of these necessities into account and give the learner access to the add-ins that may be required to access the information in the library.

Likewise, a Scenario Four user may have a variety of devices to access the information and may not know the format in which the information is coded or may want to use only a portion of the information—perhaps the audio component only. The learner may choose to listen to, instead of reading or viewing, an abstract. Learners should be able to direct libraries to download a copy to their e-mail address or to an FTP site.

In an EPSS, the learner interacts with an electronic mentor in real time. Typically, the learner engages the mentor to obtain advice on the performance of a task. While trying to complete a task, the learner encounters unknowns and asks the system for help. The system has to interpret the question and generate a response that prescribes references and training modules and then allows the learner access to the training session. For example, the learner may be an investment adviser trying to determine what long-term savings option makes the most sense for a client based on just-implemented tax law changes. The learner can provide the information to an expert system, get advice, see examples, and create a presentation to help the customer understand the recommendations. The training provided to the investment adviser then becomes presentation material for the adviser's client.

The Future of Networked Learning Environments

The challenge of creating networked learning environments is to determine what learners truly need and how to reasonably accommodate their needs. At some point in the future, all of the technological capabilities described here and more will be supported. Learners, instructors, and educational providers will then have rich options in determining how to create, navigate, and experience learning. Our early experiences with distance learning networks, the Internet, and virtual libraries will foreshadow the future networked learning environments. Simple functions such as the "bookmark" feature of the Internet browsers of today will be aggressively expanded to provide us with the ability to bookmark our journeys in an electronic world. Intelligent electronic agents that understand learner interest and requirements will assist learners in locating and navigating virtual libraries. They will be able to store learning experiences in a virtual space for learners and for others to reexperience and interact with again and again.

Networked learning environments will run the gamut from single educational provider networks to large commercial systems built on years of collaboration and partnering. There exist many challenges, both technological and pedagogical, that must be addressed on the road ahead. We will need new tools to store voice, video, and data files, facilitate finding them, and present them in forms usable with multiple systems. Tools needed include information indexing agents, search engines, expert systems, scenario builders, massive multimedia storage, and broadband multimedia networks. The networked learning environment will need to be flexible enough to accommodate rapid change. We need to start now to begin our journey on this revolutionary and evolutionary path toward this future learning environment.

Resources

Chute, A. G., Hancock, B. W., and Balthazar, L. B. "Distance Education Futures: Information Needs and Technology Options." *Performance and Instruction,* Nov.–Dec. 1991.

Chute, A. G., and Sayers, P. K. (eds.). Center for Excellence in Distance Learning Web site. [http://www.lucent.com/cedl], 1995.

Davis, S., and Botkin, J. *The Monster Under the Bed: How Business Is Mastering the Opportunity.* New York: Simon & Schuster, 1994.

Gates, B. *The Road Ahead.* New York: Viking, 1995.

Johansen, R., and others. *Groupware: Computer Support for Business Teams.* New York: Free Press, 1988.

Mehlinger, H. D. *School Reform in the Information Age*. Newtown, Pa.: Media Management, 1995.

Moore, M. G. (ed.). *Contemporary Issues in American Distance Education*. New York: Pergamon Press, 1990.

Negroponte, N. *Being Digital*. New York: Knopf, 1995.

Stolovitch, H. D., and Keeps, E. J. (eds.). *Handbook of Human Performance Technology: A Comprehensive Guide for Analyzing and Solving Performance Problems in Organizations*. San Francisco: Jossey-Bass, 1992.

Sullivan, G., and Rocco, T. *Guiding Principles for Distance Learning in a Learning Society*. Washington, D.C.: American Council on Education, 1996.

ALAN G. CHUTE *is the chief learning strategist of the Lucent Technologies Center for Excellence in Distance Learning.*

PAMELA K. SAYERS *is a distance learning specialist in the Lucent Technologies Center for Excellence in Distance Learning.*

RICHARD P. GARDNER *is a learning systems manager for AT&T Middle Market Product Learning Group.*

Part Four

Administrative Issues for the Distance Instructor

Strategies for determining the effectiveness of a distance education program are described.

Evaluating Teaching and Learning at a Distance

Michael R. Simonson

The best way to find things out is not to ask questions at all. If you fire off a question, it is like firing off a gun—bang it goes, and everything takes flight and runs for shelter. But if you sit quite still and pretend not to be looking, all the little facts will come and peck around your feet, situations will venture forth from thickets, and intentions will creep out and sun themselves on a stone; and if you are very patient, you will see and understand a great deal more than a person with a gun does [Huxley, 1982].

This marvelous quote from Huxley's *The Flame Trees of Thika* (1982) illustrates a metaphorical rationale for a major refocusing of procedures for evaluating distance education systems. Traditional evaluation models have concentrated on the empirical and quantitative procedures that have been practiced for decades (Stufflebeam and Shinkfield, 1985; Worthen and Sanders, 1987). More recently, evaluators of distance education programs have begun to propose qualitative models that include the collection of many non-numerical types of information.

This chapter discusses two approaches to distance education evaluation. First, Woodley and Kirkwood's (1986) summary of evaluation procedures will be discussed. Second, the AEIOU approach to evaluation developed by Fortune and Keith (1992), Sweeney (1995), and Sorensen (1996) will be explained. The purpose of reviewing these approaches will be to provide a foundation for evaluating distance education programs.

It is important to differentiate between theory-based research and evaluation. Hanson and Maushak (1996) have provided an excellent review of distance education literature, including research on and about distance education. Hanson summarizes distance education research as follows:

Distance education is just as effective as traditional education with regard to learner outcomes.
Distance education learners generally have more favorable attitudes toward distance education than traditional learners do, and distance learners feel that they learn as well as nondistant students.

The research clearly shows that distance education is an effective method for teaching and learning (Hanson and Maushak, 1996).

Evaluation, as contrasted to research, is the systematic investigation of the worth or merit of an object. Program evaluation is the systematic investigation of the worth of an ongoing or continuing distance education activity (Joint Committee on Standards for Educational Evaluation, 1994). This chapter discusses procedures for evaluation that assist in the improvement of the practice of distance education or that determine the worth of distance education activities. Additional information related to evaluation and distance education is available in Cyrs and Smith, 1990; Willis, 1994; Fitz-Gibbon and Morris, 1987; Worthen and Sanders, 1987; and Rossi and Freeman, 1993.

Alternative Evaluation Philosophies

Program evaluation at the Open University of Great Britain is considered to be the systematic investigation of the merit of a particular distance education program, curriculum, or teaching method and how it might be improved compared with alternatives. As part of evaluation procedures for distance education by the Open University (Woodley and Kirkwood, 1986), two alternative strategies have been merged. The first is the traditional approach, which attempts to apply the rules and procedures of the physical sciences to evaluation. The second is a more eclectic view of evaluation that incorporates qualitative and naturalistic techniques.

The traditional strategy normally includes an experiment to determine the effectiveness of a distance education project. The project is structured from its beginning with the requirements of the evaluator in mind. Carefully matched samples are picked, controls are established, and variables are selected for which comparison data will be collected. Next, objective tests of variables are selected or constructed. Data are collected before, during, and always after the instructional event or procedures. The evaluator then takes the data and prepares the evaluation report, which is submitted weeks or months later.

Recently at the Open University and elsewhere, a countermovement to this method has emerged (House, 1986). In this countermovement, evaluation activities are incorporating more naturalistic methodologies with holistic perspectives. This second perspective for evaluation uses focus groups, interviews, observations, and journals to collect evaluation information in order to obtain a rich and colorful understanding of events.

From a practical standpoint, most evaluators now use a combination of quantitative and qualitative measures. Certainly, there is a need to quantify and count. Just as certainly there is a need to understand opinions and hear perspectives.

Categories of Evaluation Information

According to Woodley and Kirkwood (1986), six categories of evaluation information can be collected about distance education activities:

1. *Measures of activity*. These measures are counts of events, people, and objects, often available from administrative records. Activity questions are ones such as

- How many courses were produced?
- How many students were served?
- How many potential students were turned away?

2. *Measures of efficiency*. Efficiency questions, also frequently available from administrative records, asked are

- How many students successfully completed the course?
- What was the average student's workload?
- How many students enrolled in additional courses?
- How much did the course cost?
- How much tuition was generated?

3. *Measures of outcomes*. Measures of adequate learning are usually considered the most important measures of outcomes of distance education activities. Often interviews with learners are used to supplement course grades in order to find students' perceptions about a distance learning activity. Mail surveys are also efficient ways to collect outcome information from distant learners. Other outcome measures include documenting the borrowing and use of courses and course materials by other institutions as an indicator of effectiveness and the enrollment by students in additional, similar courses as indicators of a course's success.

4. *Measures of program aims*. Some distance teaching programs specify their aims in terms of what and whom they intend to teach, and evaluation information is collected to establish the extent to which these aims were met. One common aim of distance education programs is to reach learners who otherwise would not be students. Surveys of learners can be used to collect this type of information.

5. *Measures of policy.* Evaluation in the policy area often takes the form of market research. Surveys of prospective students and employers can be used to determine the demand for distance education activities.

Policy evaluation can also include monitoring. Students can be surveyed to determine whether tuition is too high, whether appropriate courses are being offered, and whether there are impediments to course success, such as the lack of access to computers or the library.

Sometimes policy evaluation can be used to determine the success of experimental programs, such as those for low achievers or for those who normally are not qualified for a program. The purpose of policy evaluation is to identify procedures that are needed or that need changing and to develop new policies.

6. *Measures of organizations.* Sometimes it is important to evaluate a distance education institution in terms of its internal organization and procedures. Evaluators sometimes are asked to monitor the process of course development or program delivery to help an organization be more efficient. This category of evaluation requires on-site visits, interviews, and sometimes the use of journals by key organization leaders.

These six categories of evaluation are not used for every distance education activity. Certainly, some modest evaluation activity is almost always necessary. It is important that the activities of evaluators be matched to programmatic needs. Woodley and Kirkwood (1986) have summarized evaluation in distance education as being a fairly eclectic process that utilizes procedures that should match program needs to evaluation activities.

The AEIOU Approach

Recently, Fortune and Keith (1992), Sweeney (1995), and Sorensen (1996) have proposed the AEIOU approach for program evaluation, especially the evaluation of distance education projects. The effectiveness of this approach has been demonstrated during its use in evaluating the activities of the Iowa Distance Education Alliance, Iowa's Star Schools Project (Simonson and Schlosser, 1995b; Sorensen, 1996), a four-year statewide distance education activity. Additionally, the model has been used to evaluate a number of other innovative projects such as the Iowa Chemistry Education Alliance (1995) and the DaVinci Project: Interactive Multimedia for Art and Chemistry (Simonson and Schlosser, 1995a).

The AEIOU approach is similar to Woodley and Kirkwood's in that it is an eclectic one that uses quantitative and qualitative methodologies. It has two primary purposes as an evaluation strategy. First, the model provides formative information to the staff about the implementation of their project. Second, it provides summative information about the value of the project and its activities.

The AEIOU evaluation process provides a framework for identifying key questions necessary for effective evaluation. Some evaluation plans use only parts of the framework, while other, more comprehensive plans use all components. Presented next are examples of evaluation questions asked in comprehensive distance education projects.

Component 1: Accountability. Did the project planners do what they said they were going to do?

This is the first step in determining the effectiveness of the project and is targeted at determining whether the project's objectives and activities were completed. Evaluation questions typically center on the completion of a specific activity and often are answered yes or no. Additionally, counts of numbers of people, things, and activities are often collected.

Questions such as the following are often asked:

- Were the appropriate number of class sessions held?
- How many students were enrolled?
- How many copies of program materials were produced, and how many were distributed?

Methods used: Accountability information is often collected from project administrative records. Project leaders are often asked to provide documentation of the level of completion of each of the project's goals, objectives, and activities. Sometimes evaluators interview project staff to collect accountability data.

Component 2: Effectiveness. How well done was the project?

This component of the evaluation process attempts to place some value on the project's activities. Effectiveness questions often focus on participant attitudes and knowledge. Obviously, grades, achievement tests, and attitude inventories are measures of effectiveness. Often raters are asked to review course materials and course presentations to determine their effectiveness, and student course evaluations can be used to collect reactions from distance education participants.

Examples of questions to determine effectiveness include

- Were the inservice participants satisfied with their distance education course?
- Did the students learn what they were supposed to learn?
- Did the teachers feel adequately prepared to teach distance learners?

Methods used: Standardized measures of achievement and attitude are traditionally used to determine program effectiveness. Surveys of students and faculty can be used to ask questions related to perceptions about the appropriateness of a project or program. Focus groups (Morgan, 1988) also provide valuable information. Finally, journals are sometimes kept by project participants and then analyzed to determine the day-to-day effectiveness of an ongoing program.

Component 3: Impact. Did the project make a difference?

During this phase of the evaluation, questions focus on identifying the changes that resulted from the project's activities, and they are tied to the stated outcomes of the project. In other words, if the project had not happened, what of importance would not have occurred? A key element of measurement of impact is the collection of longitudinal data.

Impact is extremely difficult to determine because determinants of impact are difficult to identify. Often evaluators use follow-up studies to determine the impressions made on project participants, and sometimes in distance education programs learners are followed and questioned by evaluators in subsequent courses and activities.

Questions might include

- Did students register for additional distance education courses?
- Has use of the distance education system increased?
- Have policies and procedures related to the use of the distance education system been developed or changed?

Methods used: Qualitative measures provide the most to the evaluator interested in program impact. Standardized tests, record data, and surveys are sometimes used. Also, interviews, focus groups, and direct observations are used to identify a program's impact.

Component 4: Organizational Context. What structures, policies, or events in the organization or environment helped or hindered the project in accomplishing its goals?

This component of evaluation has traditionally not been important, even though evaluators have often hinted in their reports about organizational policies that either hindered or helped a program. Recently, however, distance educators have become very interested in organizational policy analysis in order to determine barriers to the successful implementation of distance education systems, especially when those systems are new activities of traditional educational organizations, such as large public universities.

The focus of this component of the evaluation is on identifying those contextual factors that contributed to, or detracted from, the project's ability to conduct activities. Usually these factors are beyond the control of the project's participants. Effective evaluation of organizational context requires the evaluator to be intimately involved with the project in order to increase awareness of the environment in which the project operates.

Questions typically addressed in evaluating organizational context include

- What factors made it difficult to implement the project?
- What contributed most to the success or failure of the project?
- What should be done differently?

Methods used: Organizational context evaluation uses interviews of key personnel, focus groups made up of those affected by a program, and document analysis that identifies policies and procedures that influence a program. Direct participation in program activities by the evaluator is also important. By participating, the evaluator is confronted directly with the organizational context in which a program exists and can comment on this context firsthand.

Component 5: Unanticipated Consequences. What changes of importance happened as a result of the project that were not expected?

This component of the AEIOU approach identifies unexpected changes that occurred as a result of the project. Effective evaluators have long been interested in reporting anecdotal information about their project or program. It is only recently that this category of information has been recognized as important. Often evaluators, especially internal evaluators who are actively involved in the project's implementation, have many opportunities to observe successes and failures during the trial-and-error process of beginning a new program. Unanticipated consequences of developing new or modified programs are a rich source of information about why some projects are successful and others are not. Central to the measurement of unanticipated outcomes is the collection of ex post facto data.

Examples of questions asked include

• Have relationships between collaborators changed in ways not expected?
• Have related, complementary projects been developed?
• Were unexpected linkages developed between groups?
• Was the distance education system used in unanticipated ways?

Methods used: Interviews, focus groups, journals, and surveys that ask for narrative information can be used to identify interesting and potentially important consequences of implementing a new program. Often, evaluators must interact with project participants on a regular basis to learn about the little successes and failures that less sensitive procedures overlook.

Conclusion

As distance education in the United States increases in importance, evaluation will continue to be a critical component of the process of improvement. Eclectic models of evaluation such as the ones advocated by Woodley and Kirkwood (1986) and Sweeney (1995) are most applicable to distance education program evaluation. Evaluators should use quantitative and qualitative procedures. Distance education programs should be accountable to their goals, should be at least as effective as alternative approaches, and should have a positive impact. Evaluators should attempt when possible to identify what organizational context supports effective distance education systems, and unanticipated events should be shared with interested readers. . . . If you are very patient, you will see and understand.

References

Cyrs, T., and Smith, F. A. *Teleclass Teaching: A Resource Guide.* (2nd ed.) Las Cruces: Center for Educational Development, New Mexico State University, 1990.

Fitz-Gibbon, C., and Morris, L. *How to Design a Program Evaluation.* San Anselmo, Calif.: Sage Press, 1987.

Fortune, J., and Keith, P. *Program Evaluation for Buchanan County Even Start.* Blacksburg: College of Education, Virginia Polytechnic Institute and State University, 1992.

Hanson, D., and Maushak, N. *Distance Education: Review of the Literature.* Ames, Iowa: Research Institute for Studies in Education, 1996.

House, E. (ed.). *New Directions in Educational Evaluation.* Lewes, England: Falmer Press, 1986.

Huxley, E. *The Flame Trees of Thika: Memories of an African Childhood.* London: Chatto and Windus, 1982.

Iowa Chemistry Education Alliance. *Iowa Chemistry Education Alliance.* Ames, Iowa: Research Institute for Studies in Education, 1995.

Joint Committee on Standards for Educational Evaluation. *The Program Evaluation Standards.* (2nd ed.) San Anselmo, Calif.: Sage Press, 1994.

Morgan, D. *Focus Groups as Qualitative Research.* San Anselmo, Calif: Sage Press, 1988.

Rossi, P., and Freeman, H. *Evaluation: A Systematic Approach.* San Anselmo, Calif.: Sage Press, 1993.

Simonson, M., and Schlosser, C. *The Da Vinci Project.* Des Moines: Iowa Computer-Using Educators Conference, 1995a.

Simonson, M., and Schlosser, C. "More than Fiber: Distance Education in Iowa." *Tech Trends,* 1995b, *40* (3), 13–15.

Sorensen, C. *Final Evaluation Report: Iowa Distance Education Alliance.* Ames, Iowa: Research Institute for Studies in Education, 1996.

Stufflebeam, D., and Shinkfield, A. *Systematic Evaluation.* Boston: Kluwer-Nijhoff, 1985.

Sweeney, J. *Vision 2020: Evaluation Report.* Ames, Iowa: Research Institute for Studies in Education, 1995.

Willis, B. (ed.). *Distance Education: Strategies and Tools.* Englewood Cliffs, N.J.: Educational Technology Publications, 1994.

Woodley, A., and Kirkwood, A. "Evaluation in Distance Learning." Paper 10. Bletchley, England: Institute of Educational Technology, Open University, 1986. (ED 304 122)

Worthen, B., and Sanders, J. *Educational Evaluation.* London: Longman, 1987.

MICHAEL R. SIMONSON is professor of education at Iowa State University.

One of the least familiar areas of concern for the distance educator is the question of copyright. What can be used, what cannot, and how to tell the difference is the subject of this chapter.

Copyright: Opportunities and Restrictions for the Teleinstructor

Janis H. Bruwelheide

Which of the following statements are true?

Distance education classes can be considered to be an extension of the traditional classroom as far as copyright situations are concerned.
Any type of visual material can be shown over a distance education network.
The copyright law is clear when it comes to distance education interpretations.
Legal penalties for copyright violations are not very costly.
It is required that the copyright notice be placed on materials; lack of notice means that they are in the public domain.
Faculty members' images and course materials may be freely used and archived for future distribution over a telecourse distribution system without concern for ownership.
It is relatively easy and not time-consuming to seek clearances and permissions from copyright owners.

You may be surprised to find that all of these statements are false. This chapter provides insights for distance educators and telecourse designers into copyright and related issues.

Copyright issues and lack of guidelines for how copyright applies to distance education are a source of increasing concern and frustration to designers and providers. Distance educators must abide by copyright law while simultaneously ensuring access to information and using technologies appropriately that, at times, seem to be in conflict with legal parameters.

Distance education courses and delivery systems have exploded onto the educational scene. New educational opportunities have resulted, but the limits

NEW DIRECTIONS FOR TEACHING AND LEARNING, no. 71, Fall 1997 © Jossey-Bass Publishers

of copyright have been stretched. Many distance education courses are highly visible and expand beyond the traditional classroom and face-to-face instructional environment, making it easier to detect copyright infringements. Distance education is viewed as a potentially lucrative field and may be seen by copyright owners as big business rather than as a nonprofit endeavor. When various media formats are combined with new materials, preexisting materials, and live lectures, the copyright situation becomes muddled. Currently, guidelines are under discussion due to the Conference on Fair Use (CONFU), which will be discussed later.

In addition to acquiring rights to *use* materials in a course, one must also acquire different rights for *transmitting* the course over various types of networks. Developers may need to acquire rights to create, reproduce, and distribute any derivative works that might result from the course. Distribution rights to send materials to distant learners may need to be obtained—prior to delivery. Course developers must think ahead about possible present and future uses, which will affect distribution, transmission, and taping. All of these factors must be considered before producing the course, or legal issues may occur after the fact and lead to additional expense. Again, one must tread carefully because current law does not provide much help and legal opinion is divided on many copyright aspects of distance education. When and if they are adopted, the CONFU guidelines will provide information as to what is permissible and what is not.

A parallel issue for distance education providers is the wide variety of intellectual property owners who can potentially be involved in a course. It is advisable to enter into written agreements with students, all contributors, faculty, and other interested parties before developing and distributing the course. Perhaps student permissions can be a condition of registration in a telecourse.

If a telecourse can be successfully sold after its initial use, then its category changes from nonprofit to profit, and fair use exemptions may not apply. Thus, designers must develop an audit sheet of what rights they need to acquire beforehand.

The NII and CONFU

The president formed the Information Infrastructure Task Force (NII) in 1993 to explore issues and develop a plan for the National Information Infrastructure. The Working Group on Intellectual Property Rights in the Electronic Environment was established to examine intellectual property issues and make recommendations concerning changes to intellectual property law and policy. The White Report, as it is called, released in September 1995, set forth the group's examination, analyses, and recommendations for each major area of intellectual property law and focused heavily on copyright law.

The Conference on Fair Use (CONFU) was convened by the working group to bring together users and copyright owners to discuss issues related to fair use and possibly develop guidelines for uses of copyrighted materials by educators and librarians. CONFU meetings began in September 1994, and talks are continuing at least through fall 1996. Five areas of educational fair use were identified for discussion and consideration by smaller working groups: multimedia, electronic reserves, distance learning, interlibrary loan, and image collections. Two additional areas were subsequently identified: software and music.

The CONFU meetings offer promise of guidelines if a majority of users and copyright owners can agree on them. To date, draft guidelines are being discussed for all areas except software and music. Originally, the groups were asked to have guidelines completed by the end of 1996. The multimedia and distance learning guidelines are nearing completion. Time will tell, however, whether there is real agreement from all sides in these areas.

Overview of Copyright

Congress has been granted the authority to regulate copyrights, and this is stated in the Constitution. These provisions are important in order to ensure authors protection for their creative work during a specified time span and at the same time to ensure societal rights and access to information. Copyright protection generally does not protect ideas per se, but it does protect the format of the expression of ideas. This protection begins the moment of creation, whether the creator registers the copyright or not. For published or unpublished works created on or after January 1, 1978, copyright protection begins at creation and lasts for fifty years after the author's death. Different time limits apply for works created prior to 1978. Works for hire, pseudonymous works, and anonymous works have copyright protection for seventy-five years from first publication or one hundred years from the year of creation, whichever expires first. On expiration of copyright, the work passes into the public domain, where it may be freely used. The owner of a copyright is granted exclusive rights, which are delineated in the section concerning Section 106 later in this chapter. Violation of these rights may result in legal action for copyright infringement and carries severe penalties.

Authors of the 1978 copyright act included language to encompass forms of expression known at that time, as well as forms still to be developed. These forms include works using any tangible means of expression, now known or later developed, from which they can be perceived, reproduced, or otherwise communicated, either directly or with the aid of a machine or device. Works of authorship include literary works; musical works, including accompanying words; dramatic works, including accompanying music; pantomimes and choreographic works; pictorial, graphic, and sculptural works; motion pictures and other audiovisual works; and sound recordings.

Newer forms of technology fall into these protected areas. Recall that the *medium* is not the issue; the *copying* of copyrighted works is the issue.

Absence of a copyright notice does not mean that the work is automatically in the public domain. Since March 1, 1989, when the United States joined the Berne Convention, affixation of the copyright notice was removed as a requirement. Thus, we must assume that if the item is "fixed" it is copyrighted, unless we are told otherwise. However, it is certainly prudent to include the notice on all materials. This action makes it easier to contact copyright owners as well as makes it difficult for infringers to claim innocent infringement. Internet materials are included. Copyright notice information usually appears on the title page or on a general, media-designated substitute, such as a title frame or credit frame on a videocassette recording. Illustrations in a work such as a collection of photographs are possibly individually copyrighted, thus requiring that each photograph copyright owner be contacted for permission.

Exclusive Rights of Copyright Holder (Section 106)

Copyright owners have certain exclusive rights. They may sell or give away these rights, whether in whole or in part. Unless permission is granted, other uses of copyrighted materials are an infringement. Owners' rights are

To reproduce the copyrighted work in copies or phonorecords
To prepare derivative works
To distribute copies or phonorecords of the copyrighted work to the public by sale or other transfer of ownership, or by rental, lease, or lending
In the case of literary, musical, dramatic, and choreographic works; pantomimes; and motion pictures and other audiovisual works, to perform the copyrighted works publicly
In the case of literary, musical, dramatic, and choreographic works; pantomimes; and pictorial, graphic or sculptural works, including the individual images of a motion picture or other audiovisual work, to display the copyrighted work publicly

Fair Use and Factors to Determine Eligibility (Section 107)

There is a provision in the copyright law for limited use of a copyrighted work without obtaining the copyright holder's permission. This use includes reproduction of portions of the work and is called "fair use" for the purposes of criticism, comment, news reporting, teaching scholarship, or research. Four factors are applied to determine whether use of a copyrighted work is a fair use:

1. The purpose and character of the use, including whether such use is of a commercial nature or is for nonprofit educational purposes
2. The nature of a copyrighted work
3. The amount and substantiality of the portion used in relation to the copyrighted work as a whole

4. The effect of the use upon the potential market for or value of the copyrighted work.

While all four factors are to be considered equally when deciding whether a use is fair, the court system has consistently demonstrated that the fourth factor appears to be more heavily weighted.

The 10 Percent Rule

A clause in section 107 that is a continual source of friction and source of this misperception is item number three in the list of factors considered for fair use: the amount and substantiality of the work. Guidelines for classroom copying and music suggest that copying 10 percent or less of the total work is fair use. However, if the amount is a "substantial portion" or represents the essence of the work and hence might affect sales if copied and distributed, then the use is not considered to be a fair use. It is not prudent to apply these guidelines to various forms of multimedia materials or anything else until appropriate guidelines are developed from the CONFU discussions.

Copyright owners hold the exclusive rights to reproduction, but they may give permission to use a work that exceeds fair use limits if asked or remunerated. The guidelines for classroom copying provide minimum guidance for the use of copyrighted materials in an educational setting. Users should affix copyright identification to copies. When in doubt, the distance educator may always ask for permission and explain the purpose. The use may be granted or negotiated subject to specific limitations and perhaps a fee payment.

Face-to-Face Teaching Activities (Section 110)

One of the most frustrating parts of the current copyright act for distance educators is Section 110, which exempts instructors and pupils involved in "face-to-face" instruction in a nonprofit educational institution from copyright liability, so that any part of a work may be displayed or performed in class. It is assumed that copies of audiovisual works used are lawfully made copies or originals. Students and teacher must be present simultaneously in the same general areas, although not necessarily in sight of each other. Some legal opinion has interpreted this situation to mean that the activity can occur on the same physical plant as long as the buildings are joined together. When in doubt about using copyrighted materials, an instructor should ask permission. Permission is not extended to transmitting these materials via networks such as interactive video or satellite without the copyright holder's approval. Attorneys for various distance education organizations within higher education are very divided on this issue, so readers should ask their counsel for clarification and support and make sure that a policy statement exists. Some attorneys consider certain types of materials and delivery mechanisms, such as interactive television (compressed video) to be covered, or at least defensible, under Section 110, the classroom exemption. They believe that 110(2)(C)ii may provide some protection for course delivery to certain groups of adult learners in remote sites. The section reads " . . . performance of a nondramatic literary or musical work or display of a work, by or in the course of a transmission if . . . (C) the transmission is made primarily for (ii) reception by persons to whom the transmission is directed because their disabilities or other special circumstances prevent their attendance in classrooms or similar places normally devoted to instruction. . . ."

There are, however, equal opinions to the effect that very little copyrighted material may be transmitted or broadcast over a distance education network without proper written permission or licensing agreements.

A concern with many distance learning situations is the possible recording at either site of a class delivered via interactive video or satellite transmission. Such recording might be for the purposes of critiquing the session or viewing by an absent student. While many of the materials that might be recorded could come under fair use, recording the transmission of copyrighted media would not be allowable without permission or licensing. There is nothing in this section of the act that gives permission to tape at a remote site for archival or review purposes. Again, it is hoped that the CONFU guidelines will provide parameters.

Suggestions for Distance Educators

Until guidelines for distance learning are available from CONFU, what can be done to avoid problems? Distance educators who are concerned may wish to consider these ideas:

Engage the support of the organizational governing body such as the college or university system headquarters office to develop a copyright policy and a manual and make sure it is adopted and implemented. A small team comprising representatives from various factions should be assembled to develop the document. Several good policies are available from sites on the Internet listed in the Resources section at the end of this chapter.

Provide training in order to develop awareness and explain the policy so that all parties are informed.

Ask permission from copyright holders.

Understand the copyright provisions, but realize that there is educational copying that is legitimate; the envelope should be pushed and common sense applied.

Place copyright credit on legally made copies.

Think about the current and future settings in which the use will occur. Think ahead and anticipate all possible problems before designing and distributing a telecourse. Conduct an audit.

Know how to help instructors locate legitimate alternatives (for example, selection aids, sources of clearing services, clip art clearinghouses).

Develop a form letter for requesting permission from copyright holders for various media formats and develop a centralized tracking system to maintain the paper trail.

Label equipment that can be used for copying with restriction notices.

Facilitate return of permission slips by including two copies of the letter and a self-addressed envelope. Call to identify the appropriate person or department that can grant permission, and address the letter accordingly. A person filling the purchase order does not have the authority to grant permissions.

Develop a blanket permissions statement for videotaping and transmitting, for example, and make it a condition of student enrollment in a class. Consider the same for a computer conferencing class where "transcripts" may be kept. Be aware of privacy issues, however.

Resources

Bruwelheide, J. H. "Copyright Concerns for Distance Educators." In B. Willis (ed.), *Distance Education: Strategies and Tools.* Englewood Cliffs, N.J.: Educational Technology Publications, 1994.

Bruwelheide, J. H. *The Copyright Primer* (2nd ed.) Chicago: American Library Association, 1995.

Bruwelheide, J. H. "Copyright and Distance Education: Issues for Librarians and Practitioners." *Library Acquisitions: Practice and Theory,* 1996, 21 (1), pp. 52–65.

Bruwelheide, J. H. "Myths and Misperceptions" (working title). In L. Gasaway (ed.), *Copyright Growing Pains,* in press.

Pisacreta, E. A. "Distance Learning and Intellectual Property Protection." *Educational Technology,* 1993, 33 (4), 42–44.

Salomon, K. "Copyright Issues and Distance Learning." *Teleconference,* 1993, 12 (1), pp. 18–21.

United States Code, Public Law 94–553, 90 Stat. 2541.

U.S. Department of Commerce. *Intellectual Property and the National Information Infrastructure.* (also know as the White Report) Washington, D.C.: GPO, 1995.

Internet Resources

A variety of materials dealing with copyright are available on the Internet for information or downloading. Listed below are two sources that are very good and that contain pointers to additional resources.

Copyright Management Center [http://lcweb.loc.gov] or [http://www.loc.gov].

Fair Use Center [http://fairuse.stanford.edu].

Janis H. Bruwelheide is professor of education, health, and human development at Montana State University-Bozeman.

The transformation of the library from a repository of printed material to a digital library serving as a complete information center where distance learners in this dynamic environment can find support for their educational aspirations is discussed.

Distance Learning and the Digital Library: Transforming the Library into an Information Center

Roberta L. Derlin, Edward Erazo

Distance learning continues to proliferate and expand educational opportunities. The rapid development of information technology now permits service delivery options for distance learning that were previously unimaginable (Bates, 1995; Miller and Wolf, 1992), and the wealth and sophistication of telecommunications options available today is radically altering traditional concepts and methods of educating (Hammer, 1994). Through technology, distance learning enhances opportunities for interaction, cooperative learning, and the formation of communities of learners rather than relying on traditional face-to-face lecture and query instructional strategies. Distance learning is a means of creating educational unification, connecting people who may be physically, socially, and/or culturally distant from one another but who are unified in active learning communities by mastery of a shared body of knowledge and common educational goals and aspirations.

The Library and Mastery of a Shared Body of Knowledge

Traditionally, the library has supported learners in their efforts to achieve mastery of a shared body of knowledge through three mechanisms: (1) access to printed material and a limited selection of other media such as records and films, (2) assistance in the search for appropriate printed material related to specific topics of interest, and (3) retrieval of printed material for the learner's use. As a repository of printed material, however, the traditional library was challenged in performing these functions because it was largely place- and time-bound, providing access to a collection of printed material at a specific site during established hours of operation or through relatively time-consuming interlibrary loan services. No matter how finely honed the search skills of the librarian or student, access was limited by factors influencing the magnitude of the collection, such as budget or the interests of faculty and library book buyers, and retrieval was limited to the specific site or burdened by the time required to process interlibrary loan requests. With the exception of relatively limited telephone services, travel to the library location was necessary to obtain any service at all.

Public Pressure for Library Transformation Through Technology

Representative surveys on library usage suggest that library patrons—including distance learners—are interested in technology and the use of computers as a means to pursue knowledge. As early as 1978, a Gallup survey on library usage suggested that 56 percent of library patrons were interested in having the library offer computers to search for information or books. In 1987, library patrons were similarly more likely than nonvisitors to think that having a home computer would be useful. Survey results in 1991 indicated that library patrons were more likely to own a home computer than nonvisitors, while on-line services to gather information were considered to be very valuable resources by library patrons and nonvisitors alike. This assessment was most prevalent among college graduates, but people who had not completed high school also indicated a substantial interest in using the technology to access information. In addition, people in poverty and minorities were among those most likely to value the use of home computers for information (Westin and Finger, 1991). Such broadly based evidence of interest in using technology to access information and acquire knowledge has been one source of pressure for library transformation.

The Realization of Public Interest

As access to information through electronic means continues to increase, the public's interest in technology as a means to master knowledge is being realized. The traditional reliance on print media is gradually being eroded, and the learning environment is becoming more and more technologically diverse and complex. The educational goals and aspirations of distance learners must be supported through expanded and technologically sophisticated services that will not only identify information sources but also develop them.

Just as the Internet and World Wide Web have eliminated the physical distance between many traditional repository libraries, so can in-home computers eliminate the physical distance between the individual and the information's resident location. As physical distance is being minimized as a limitation in the acquisition of knowledge, the interactions between human and computer continue to be challenging and, for some humans, troubling. Fortunately, the technological environment is getting ever more user-friendly. Searching World Wide Web sites using browsers such as Netscape provides users with precise search capabilities and access to information incorporating graphics and motion pictures (animation). The introduction of sound and pictures magnifies the educational experience and supports the varied learning styles of individual learners. As the relationship between humans and technologies continues to develop in supportive and exciting ways, both distance learning opportunities and information access will continue to expand and improve through the development of learning modules available through computers at the information centers of the future (Murray, 1995).

However, there is currently a plethora of on-line information services, and as access continues to grow at an exponential rate, so does its complexity. The challenge faced by distance learners pursuing knowledge at the present is not how to access some or enough information, but how effectively to use and manage existing technologies to limit access. Acquiring only the most relevant information, or at least a manageable amount of information, to facilitate the process of transforming data and information into mastery of a shared body of knowledge is a continual challenge for learners. Teaching patrons how to effectively apply the increasingly sophisticated search methods available on-line will be an important function in the digital library. For this reason, strong library instruction programs, both formal and informal, will be a key concern for information centers.

Future Challenges to Library Transformation

As distance learners are challenged to effectively use and manage technologies for distance learning, the current trends in library transformation and technology development will persist. The Internet will continue to provide an unparalleled state of worldwide connectivity among diverse people, and access to it will increasingly extend to people in their homes, vehicles, post offices, information centers, malls, offices, and educational centers. Libraries and other resources on-line will be challenged to provide more comprehensive services to more broadly based and active learning communities that will arise through expanded distance learning opportunities.

The World Wide Web will continue to grow and will become a major publishing medium. The writer's traditional reliance on the word will be challenged, and writers will increasingly incorporate visual images, motion, and auditory stimuli to enhance the impact of the communication. Individuals will be able to self-publish their views on the Internet more broadly than ever before and in a format far more accessible to others than traditional printed media. World Wide Web celebrities will arise and be internationally known for their work.

Current legal principles of copyright and fair use will be challenged and revised. Libraries currently provide a mechanism to control access and distribution of copyright-protected materials (Gasaway and Wiant, 1994). With advances in technology, the ability of users to access, download, and manipulate on-line information for personal, professional, and academic purposes will require alternative mechanisms to establish control of digital text (Bloch and Hesse, 1993). With a profusion of self-publication through the World Wide Web and increasing numbers of periodicals available on-line, it is anticipated that the period of time before texts enter the public domain will be shortened.

The ability to receive vast amounts of electronic mail as well as on-line periodical publications every day will require the ability to screen and sort incoming information and will be a major area of technology development. Being able to separate the wheat from the chaff and identify the information worthy of attention as educational goals and aspirations are pursued will be an increasingly important skill in distance learning. Instructions to patrons through learning modules available from digital libraries will be an important means of eliminating information overload.

The Future Library as Information Center

The future library as information center will have an expanded role in providing educational activities, services, materials, and opportunities for human interaction. The library will provide technology and information literacy training as well as training in critical thinking skills, the process of selecting and using information to create new knowledge and master existing knowledge. The library will also develop customized multimedia learning modules to present these educational services to faculty and distance learners on demand through distance learning or in face-to-face on-site or on-line interactive learning environments.

Future libraries will continue to incorporate existing and improved technologies in new and creative ways. An example is the scanning technology most commonly utilized today in the fax machine. Currently, scanning technology can take up to a minute to put a printed page on-line. In the future, scanning speed will improve and scanners will be used not only to transform printed material, but also to deliver information directly to the distance learner's personal computer. Scanners will also be used to search for key words or phrases within texts of books and databases to make published works available for study. This vision of the future is currently being realized by the success of Project Gutenberg, which has made full-text copy of a large number of classic, religious, and children's books, as well as poetry and historical documents available by computer (Crawford and Gorman, 1995). Library production of customized materials and direct delivery of these materials to distance learners through enhanced technology will increase the number of people using the services and expand participation in future learning communities.

The future information centers will be distance learner centered, and these distance learners will be more broadly representative of the world's diversity: elder and youthful learners; well-educated and less-well-educated learners; learners who live or have lived in poverty and those who are materially well endowed; and minority and nonminority learners (Riggs and Sabine, 1988). This expanded diversity in learning communities will allow the library as future information center to realize more fully its historic role as a social institution created to provide equitable access to knowledge in a free society (Scholars and Research Libraries, 1990).

The future information center will be neither place- nor time-bound. Multiuser access to databases and reference materials such as dictionaries and government documents on-line will improve user access. Reference collections and other services will be available twenty-four hours a day, as will on-line reading rooms providing access to periodicals and journals. Use of on-line study rooms, descendants of Internet "chat" rooms, will be expanded and will increase on-line interaction within distance learning communities. Distance learners and librarians alike will be able to work fully from a remote location. Traditional research, reference, and print support of curriculum development in educational centers will incorporate pictures and sound to benefit individual learning styles, and technology advances that allow us to see and hear one another, such as CU-SeeMe, will make on-line communication among distance learners or between distance learners and librarians more personal.

Despite increasing personalization of communications on-line and increasing technological sophistication in interactive distance learning, the human need and desire for face-to-face communication in proximity will be recognized by these future information centers. They will provide facilities for distance learners to gather, with or without their machines, for learning and social exchanges in support of the development of enriched learning, social, and cultural communities.

The Future Role of Librarians as Information Specialists.

As the digital library is transformed into the future information center, so will the role of the librarian be radically transformed. It will change from the traditional search-and-retrieval role to one with increased responsibility: to provide guidance in the use of technology, to access information from varied locations (Bloch and Hesse, 1993), and to collaborate with faculty to develop learning opportunities for distance learners (Murray, 1995).

Through technology innovation, future information specialists will work more closely with faculty and distance learners to provide materials and reference as well as instructional services either on- or off-line. This greater collaboration will contribute to the trend to develop academic teams of library personnel, faculty, and distance learners, which will facilitate distance and cooperative learning and influence librarians in their work (Riggs and Sabine, 1988). Librarians have already demonstrated the ability to embrace new opportunities to redefine their roles, taking a proactive stance and grasping the technological innovations that are so rapidly changing their libraries (Latham, Slade, and Budnick, 1991). However, information specialists will encounter mounting tension between pressure from distance learners for more information faster and pressure to sift and winnow an overabundance of information. It will be important for these future information specialists to remain committed to assisting in information selection without restricting access to information based on personal opinions or preferences.

Library Transformation: To Be or Not to Be

The future is unpredictable, and ambiguity surrounds the realization of the digital library envisioned in this chapter. Current library personnel and administrators struggle daily with a myriad of unanticipated developments, emerging technological advances, and various operating and policy concerns that may either hinder, facilitate, or radically alter library transformation. It is important to identify some of the challenges that library personnel and administrators face at the present in realizing the digital library of the future in the long run.

Technology Issues.   There is a continuing debate among leaders in library administration about how to realize library transformation in an environment of such great uncertainty. How much reliance should remain on printed media? How will the use of electronic information be preserved in the face of system failure? How much space (physical or digital) should be devoted to storing information, and for how long?

The continued free access envisioned in library transformation in this chapter may be inhibited by political, social, and cultural concerns emerging about the Internet. More and more frequently, people are expressing concern about the content of information available on the Internet and a desire to achieve control over that content and access to it. Just how successful attempts to regulate the Internet will be is not known, but legislation is pending at the federal level targeted at some of these concerns. The magnitude of regulation that will be achieved, the ability to enforce regulatory attempts, and how such regulations will ultimately influence the digital library of the future are also unknowns.

Information Issues.   As mentioned previously, it is anticipated that traditional copyright policies and enforcement mechanisms will be altered. However, even broader questions about knowledge production and ownership are being raised, and the future resolution of these questions cannot be determined at present. Access to information and the ability to readily alter information challenge traditional concepts of knowledge production and ownership.

These worrisome scenarios are indicative of the magnitude of social and political concerns surrounding technological advances. The economic concerns that seem so troubling now, on the other hand, can gradually be resolved over time because the costs associated with technology have consistently declined. However, if regulation or new policies become burdensome, technological advances would be slowed and the realization of the information center of the future would be delayed.

Future librarians as information specialists must be prepared to do their part to realize the transformation of the digital library into the future information center to meet the increasing demands of distance learners. Only by learning these new technologies and skills—such as the World Wide Web/Internet and instructional design—and keeping pace with new technological developments in distance learning can future information specialists accomplish this. The success of future information centers depends on it.

References

Bates, A. W. *Technology, Open Learning, and Distance Education.* New York: Routledge, 1995.

Bloch, R. H., and Hesse, C. (eds.). *Future Libraries.* Berkeley: University of California Press, 1993.

Crawford, W., and Gorman, M. *Future Libraries: Dreams, Madness, and Reality.* Chicago: American Library Association, 1995.

Gasaway, L. N., and Wiant, S. K. *Libraries and Copyright: A Guide to the Copyright Law in the 1990s.* Washington, D.C.: Special Library Association, 1994.

Hammer, K. G. "Off-Campus Library Services and the Impact of NCA Accreditation." Master's research paper, Kent State University, Kent, Ohio, 1994. (ED 367 849)

Latham, S., Slade, A. L., and Budnick, C. *Library Services for Off-Campus and Distance Education: An Annotated Bibliography.* Ottawa, Ontario: Canadian Library Association, 1991.

Miller, R. B., and Wolf, M. T. (eds). *Thinking Robots, an Aware Internet, and Cyberpunk Librarians: The 1992 LITA President's Program: Presentations by Hans Moravec, Bruce Sterling, and David Brin.* Chicago: American Library Association, 1992.

Murray, R. B. *Accessing New Learning Environments.* Philadelphia: Thomas Jefferson University, 1995. Videotape.

Riggs, D. E., and Sabine, G. A. *Libraries in the '90s: What the Leaders Expect.* Phoenix, AZ: Oryx Press, 1988.

Scholars and Research Libraries in the Twenty-First Century: American Council of Learned Societies, New York, April 27, 1990. New York: American Council of Learned Societies, 1990.

Westin, A. F., and Finger, A. L. *Using the Public Library in the Computer Age: Present Patterns, Future Possibilities.* Chicago: American Library Association, 1991.

ROBERTA L. DERLIN *is associate professor for educational management and development at New Mexico State University.*

EDWARD ERAZO *is assistant professor of library science, New Mexico State University.*

*The case for comprehensive information and support services for
distance education is made in this chapter. Consideration in designing
such a service system and developing opportunities and challenges
are outlined.*

Managing Information Resources and Services in a Distance Environment

Robert S. Tolsma

Institutions of learning are information- and communications-based organizations. The media for communicating information have expanded from simple print, voice, and face-to-face communications to include fax, voice mail, computer-assisted instruction, e-mail, video, and other technologies, and these technologies have become more central to the mission of education. Asynchronous forms of interpersonal communications such as computer conferencing move the very substance of education, the human discourse of learning, into a technology-mediated environment. To an increasing degree, technology is used to provide a wide range of services formerly provided through direct personal contact. Managing information resources now means managing access not only to data but to academic discourse and to various student and technical support services as well. This technological environment where academic discourse takes place and where services are rendered needs to be managed, and faculty, staff, and students need to be trained to use it effectively.

The management challenge is even greater in a distance education environment. Students at a distance, and faculty, need access to nearly all of the corpus of information resources and services that is available to their campus-based peers, and in addition they need information about the policies and procedures that differ for distance students. Many students take a mix of campus and distance courses and must often understand how to navigate across different, even contradictory, policies and procedures for each. They are furthermore often asked to integrate local information resources and services within their learning experience, including local libraries, tutors, or proctors for exams. Managing the information flow and service arrangements in such a complex set of relationships is a difficult task for students, faculty, and staff alike.

Despite the complexity of providing to distance students the full spectrum of information resources and services provided to those in campus-based programs, there are good reasons for developing a system to do so. The primary reason is that such a system is essential to implement and support sound teaching and learning practices. A recent report by the Education Commission of the States, *Making Quality Count in Undergraduate Education* (1995), cited twelve principles of good practice that research indicates are critical in improving student performance and satisfaction. Among the most critical for distance education are assessment and prompt feedback, collaboration, and out-of-class contact with faculty. Without an effective system to support communications among faculty, staff, and students, students cannot receive prompt feedback, will find collaboration with each other difficult, and will feel uninvolved with faculty teaching the course.

A robust information and service system is increasingly recognized as an important criterion in assessing the quality of distance education. As early as 1988, the boards of both EDUCOM and CAUSE, the larger higher education membership organizations in educational and information technology, adopted guidelines to be used by accrediting agencies to evaluate campus information resources (CAUSE/EDUCOM, 1988). Even these early guidelines recognized the need for readily available information technology resources and training for "students in continuing education and off-campus programs." More recently, the Western Cooperative for Educational Telecommunications developed "Principles of Good Practice for Electronically Offered Academic Degree and Certificate Programs" (1995). These principles, which have been adopted by several organizations, include a strong emphasis on information resources and support services for both faculty and students.

Even assuming adequate resources and a strong commitment to a comprehensive system of information and student services, there are no universal recipes for providing them. In some programs, students study independently at home, receive a print-based "course-in-a-box," and communicate with instructors through the U.S. postal system. By contrast, other programs attempt to replicate the campus classroom at a distance through two-way video. Instructors may even alternate the location from which they broadcast the class. The type of information and service system that can provide resources for a student and faculty member working in the replicated classroom environment, in facilities owned by the institution and supported by local employees of the institution, is unlikely to be the same as that required for the student studying at home.

Moreover, it is not only the characteristics of the physical environment or even the technological differences in delivery systems that differentiate the support needs of one distance education program from another. Communications and support systems should accommodate the academic and instructional design decisions they are intended to implement. To the degree that those programmatic decisions differ, the system that supports them should differ also. Academic programs with an emphasis on writing across the curriculum, classroom assessment, student portfolios, competency-based curricula, and many other instructional methods each place unique burdens on any information and service system.

Despite this variety and the constantly changing nature of distance education environments, there are recurring issues that every education provider needs to address, and the choices that institutions make regarding them suggest the feature of the information and service system they need to establish to accommodate their own environmental, technological, and programmatic parameters.

Instructional Objectives, Strategies, and Outcomes

What are the instructional objectives, strategies, and outcomes that are important to you on an institutional, program, or course level that require some kind of information resources or service support? Realizing objectives such as having students acquire an understanding of and appreciation for human diversity or the virtues of public service, employing strategies such as classroom assessment or collaborative learning, or requiring demonstration of outcomes through student portfolios or competency testing all place different burdens and challenges on an information and service system. Being clear about the instructional objectives, strategies, and outcomes you need a system to support is essential for planning.

Service Responsibilities

What organization(s) should have operational responsibility for services to distance students and faculty? Should the services offered in your programs be provided in whole or in part by using the existing campus service system, should you create a separate service system for distance education, or should you outsource responsibility to an external party?

Using the existing campus service system certainly has some obvious advantages. Systems for providing campus-based students access to the information and services they need through computer-based campus information systems are getting better, and many are becoming easily accessible through the World Wide Web. The University of Maryland's on-line student information service called Testudu is a good example ("Testudu," 1996). As institutions increasingly recognize the value of providing integrated comprehensive and accessible student services, extending campus processes of service provision may prove to be more adequate for distance education than has been the case.

Although outsourcing campus services is not new—vendor-run campus bookstores and food services have been common for decades—interest in outsourcing arrangements is growing. For example, many computing departments are seeking arrangements with vendors to operate campus modem pools for Internet access. Distance education programs too have developed successful relationships with external service providers. America Online's Electronic University provides Brevard Community College and many others with an on-line computer learning environment for their distance education classes, and Walden University has contracted with the Indiana University libraries to provide student library services ("Walden University Library Services," 1996).

There are times when neither extending the campus system nor outsourcing your services is the best option. The Education Network of Maine, with students from all seven campuses of the University of Maine system, many of whom took courses from more than one institution in the same semester, found that providing a convenient and integrated set of student services was possible only by developing a single point of contact for service information for all of these courses and programs through a new toll-free Teleservice operation.

Quality Standards

What quality standards do you want your information and service system to observe in achieving the aforementioned strategies? For example, what should be the maximum time a student has to wait for a book ordered from the library, or what is the longest time a faculty member should have to wait to get a class list of distance students? How long should students have to wait for a reply to an e-mail inquiry, and what should be their maximum wait in a phone queue? Choices regarding standards obviously affect the system design and technologies you require. If your standard is to have students receive the results of their tests within twenty-four hours of when they are graded, using the U.S. postal service for delivering that information is probably not going to meet that objective.

Competing Service Values

Nearly every institution will face the task of selecting from competing service values. For example, programs need to decide what value they place on personal service and must select the pass-off points between providing personal service and technologically mediated service. Are phone calls, for example, answered by an automated attendant or a human voice?

Other service value questions are more difficult. Easy access to technology is one of the key factors determining student satisfaction and success with a technology-mediated course, yet providing equally easy access is a difficult standard. What deviations from it are acceptable? Should you use features such as audio on your Web site, knowing that students who do not have sound cards in their computers will not be able to take advantage of it? And when you do start putting information services on-line for students, will you also continue to provide duplicate avenues to these resources and services through print or in-person services, particularly where computer access and aptitude might not be equal for all participants?

Whether to provide duplicate sources of information and service is a question not only of access, however, but also of responsibility. Telephone companies long ago discovered that a large percentage of calls for directory assistance are from people who have access to the same information in a phone book but find looking in the book less convenient than calling. How much responsibility will you assume for developing and making information available, and how much will you put on the student or faculty member? As Lucinda Roy noted in a recent presentation, support staff often feel like and are treated like "indentured servants" (1996). It is difficult to find institutional agreement on the line between providing good service and assuming responsibilities that would be better discharged by other parties.

Nuts and Bolts of Academic Logistics

The questions to be answered here are not mysterious. What information resources (for example, policies and procedures) do you need to create? Who is responsible for creating, maintaining, and updating the information participants need? What are the communication and information flow processes for making this information available?

A large distance education program can generate tremendous information demands and quite a complex information system. The problem of managing it is easy to underestimate. Procedures followed on campus are seldom fully adequate for distance programs, yet deviations from them can easily go undocumented and prove an enigma to participants.

As more information resources become available in digital form, keeping that information current and accurate becomes a major endeavor. Even a cursory examination of university Web sites will reveal examples of outdated information. Technologies for dynamically presenting the most accurate information as it is created are improving, but developing procedures for the maintenance of information will remain a key requirement.

Costs and Benefits

Ascertaining the costs and benefits of information and service options is essential to allocating your service resources effectively. Many institutions do not have extensive experience or effective tools to do so, particularly if services are delivered through technological means. Although technology is often seen as a cost-saving device, we know that it is not always so. For example, technology often requires a certain level of usage before it is more cost-effective than having a person provide the information or service. Calculating the true cost is only the first and probably the easiest step. Evaluating the effectiveness or benefits of technology for students is an even more difficult task.

Those tasks are beginning to be addressed. The Annenberg/Corporation for Public Broadcasting is sponsoring a project called FLASHLIGHT aimed at this problem. This project will produce an item bank of questions for creating evaluation instruments to assess the effectiveness of the use of technology. A cost model that institutions can use to calculate the true cost of their educational technology implementations is also being developed (Flashlight Project, 1996).

Technology Choices

Which technologies should we use? Fax-back systems, computer bulletin boards, and the World Wide Web can provide unattended access to information. Help lines, e-mail, voice mail, computer conferencing, and computer-based "chat" programs can provide either immediate or time-delayed interactive access to service providers. Help-desk software can help service providers track and analyze service requests.

Conceptually, the selection of technology is a training question. Different technologies are clearly more appropriate for different environments and for supporting different instructional strategies, and are more consonant with some sets of service values than are other technologies. Clarity on the other above-mentioned issues will go a long way toward identifying the criteria that must direct the selection of technology and will help you make that selection before the technology you are considering is obsolete.

As these service decisions indicate, creating an information and service system involves orchestrating the interplay of physical environment; human resources; and technological, programmatic, and fiscal constraints, along with a set of values about what constitutes a supportive learning environment for students. Current trends hold forth the promise that better service solutions will be forthcoming. Their importance is certainly gaining recognition. Researchers are finding that "the learning experience embraces all of the actions which occur from the point of contact with the institution to the point of departure" (Murgatroyd, 1996, pp. 6–7) and is not limited to the instructional classroom. Institutional policy statements (OSSHE, 1996) voice strong commitment to providing comprehensive services to students at a distance, and promoting such services is becoming a priority for funding sources. The Fund for the Improvement of Post-Secondary Education (FIPSE) recently awarded a grant to the Colorado Electronic Community College to design high-quality instructional and student services materials called "utility educationware," and it awarded another to the Western Cooperative for Educational Telecommunications (WCET) to help institutions, including the new Western Governors University, implement innovative approaches to services. Technology that is easier to use, voice-activated systems, and desktop video promise to extend the range of services provided through telecommunications. Expanded student access to computing will make it more available.

Despite this promising future, very large challenges remain. Technological innovation, public policy demands for efficiency and accountability, and competitive pressures from an opening educational marketplace stand poised to drive a period of great pedagogical and organizational experimentation that will challenge institutions to create integrated, easily accessed, and high-quality services in a complex multi-institutional environment. Creative students will drive market demands for innovative programs of study that are individualized to their particular academic aspirations, that draw upon the resources of many institutions, that recognize and credit the value of their previous studies, that accommodate their domestic and work scheduling needs, and that result in learning that is publicly verifiable to a greater extent than current accreditation and credentialing processes commonly afford. The information resources and student support services that will be needed to support these programmatic features are largely undeveloped at most institutions. Elements of what would be required in an integrated multi-institutional service system can be seen in the "credit bank" being developed by the Open Learning Agency (1996), in the Education Network of Maine's Teleservice operation (1996), and in regional student service centers that are being developed by OSSHE (1996) and others. How these services will address the tension between integrating information and student services and preserving the organizational autonomy and diversity of their participating institutions is still unfolding. Technology may well create a situation in which the student market itself determines what policies and practices have any value, empowering students in ways that barriers of time and geography have prevented before, to vote with tuition dollars for institutions with the most supportive learning environments.

References

CAUSE/EDUCOM. *Evaluation Guidelines for Institutions Information Technology Resources.* Boulder, Colo.: CAUSE/EDUCOM, 1988. See an updated (1995) version of these guidelines by the Higher Education Information Resources Alliance of ARL, CAUSE, and EDUCOM at http://cause-www.colorado.edu/collab/heirapapers/hei2000.html.

Education Commission of the States. *Making Quality Count in Undergraduate Education.* Denver: Education Commission of the States, 1995.

Education Network of Maine. [http://www.enm.maine.edu] 1996.

"Flashlight Project." [http://www.learner.org/content/ed/strat/eval/evalflash.html] 1996.

Murgatroyd, S. "QFD: A New Technology of Instructional Design for Distance Education." Unpublished paper, 1996.

Open Learning Agency. [http://olax.ola.bc.ca/stuserv/creditbank.html] 1996.

OSSHE (Oregon State System of Higher Education). "Distance Education Policy Framework." [http://www.osshe.edu/dist-learn/dist-pol.htm], 1996.

Roy, L. *The Virtual College: Groping Forward.* Presentation at Seminars on Academic Computing '96, Snowmass, Colo., 1996.

"Testudu." College Park: University of Maryland [http://www.testudo.umd.edu], 1996.

"Walden University Library Services." [gopher://win.waldenu.edu:70/00/.comp-sup/Library/ Walden percent20University percent20Library percent20Liaison], 1996.

Western Cooperative for Educational Telecommunications. "Principles of Good Practice for Electronically Offered Academic Degree and Certificate Programs." Denver: Western Cooperative for Educational Telecommunications, [http://www.wiche.edu/telecom/principles.htm], 1995.

ROBERT S. TOLSMA *is executive director of the Greater Rochester Area University Center, Minnesota.*

INDEX

ORDERING INFORMATION

NEW DIRECTIONS FOR TEACHING AND LEARNING is a series of paperback books that presents ideas and techniques for improving college teaching, based both on the practical expertise of seasoned instructors and on the latest research findings of educational and psychological researchers. Books in the series are published quarterly in Spring, Summer, Fall, and Winter and are available for purchase by subscription as well as by single copy.

SUBSCRIPTIONS cost $54.00 for individuals (a savings of 35 percent over single-copy prices) and $90.00 for institutions, agencies, and libraries. Please do not send institutional checks for personal subscriptions. Standing orders are accepted. Prices subject to change. (For subscriptions outside of North America, add $7.00 for shipping via surface mail or $25.00 for air mail. Orders *must be prepaid* in U.S. dollars by check drawn on a U.S. bank or charged to VISA, MasterCard, or American Express.)

SINGLE COPIES cost $22.00 plus shipping (see below) when payment accompanies order. California, New Jersey, New York, and Washington, D.C., residents please include appropriate sales tax. Canadian residents add GST and any local taxes. Billed orders will be charged shipping and handling. No billed shipments to post office boxes. (Orders from outside North America *must be prepaid* in U.S. dollars by check drawn on a U.S. bank or charged to VISA, MasterCard, or American Express.)

SHIPPING (SINGLE COPIES ONLY): $30.00 and under, add $5.50; to $50.00, add $6.50; to $75.00, add $7.50; to $100.00, add $9.00; to $150.00, add $10.00.

DISCOUNTS FOR QUANTITY ORDERS are available. Please write to the address below for information.

ALL ORDERS must include either the name of an individual or an official purchase order number. Please submit your order as follows:
    Subscriptions: specify series and year subscription is to begin
    Single copies: include individual title code (such as TL54)

MAIL ORDERS TO:
    Jossey-Bass Publishers
    350 Sansome Street
    San Francisco, CA 94104-1342

    PHONE subscription or single-copy orders toll-free at (888) 378-2537 or at (415) 433-1767 (toll call).

    FAX orders toll-free to: (800) 605-2665

FOR SUBSCRIPTION SALES OUTSIDE OF THE UNITED STATES, CONTACT:
    any international subscription agency or Jossey-Bass directly.

OTHER TITLES AVAILABLE IN THE
NEW DIRECTIONS FOR TEACHING AND LEARNING SERIES
Robert J. Menges, Editor-in-Chief
Marilla D. Svinicki, Associate Editor

TL70   Approaches to Teaching Non-Native English Speakers Across
        the Curriculum, David L. Sigsbee, Bruce W. Speck, Bruce Maylath
TL69   Writing to Learn: Strategies for Assigning and Responding to Writing Across
        the Disciplines, Mary Deane Sorcenelli, Peter Elbow
TL68   Bringing Problem-Based Learning to Higher Education: Theory and Practice,
        LuAnn Wilkerson, Wim H. Gijselaers
TL67   Using Active Learning in College Classes: A Range of Options for Faculty,
        Tracey E. Sutherland, Charles C. Bonwell
TL66   Ethical Dimensions of College and University Teaching: Understanding
        and Honoring the Special Relationship Between Teachers and Students,
        Linc. Fisch
TL65   Honoring Exemplary Teaching, Marilla D. Svinicki, Robert J. Menges
TL64   Disciplinary Differences in Teaching and Learning: Implications for Practice,
        Nira Hativa, Michele Marincovich
TL63   Understanding Self-Regulated Learning, Paul R. Pintrich
TL62   Teaching Through Academic Advising: A Faculty Perspective,
        Alice G. Reinarz, Eric R. White
TL61   Fostering Student Success in Quantitative Gateway Courses, Joanne Gainen,
        Eleanor W. Willemsen
TL60   Supplemental Instruction: Increasing Achievement and Retention,
        Deanna C. Martin, David R. Arendale
TL59   Collaborative Learning: Underlying Processes and Effective Techniques,
        Kris Bosworth, Sharon J. Hamilton
TL58   Interdisciplinary Studies Today, Julie Thompson Klein, William G. Doty
TL57   Mentoring Revisited: Making an Impact on Individuals and Institutions,
        Marie A. Wunsch
TL56   Student Self-Evaluation: Fostering Reflective Learning, Jean MacGregor
TL55   Developing Senior Faculty as Teachers, Martin J. Finkelstein,
        Mark W. LaCelle-Peterson
TL54   Preparing Faculty for the New Conceptions of Scholarship, Laurie Richlin
TL53   Building a Diverse Faculty, Joanne Gainen, Robert Boice
TL52   Promoting Diversity in College Classrooms: Innovative Responses for the
        Curriculum, Faculty, and Institutions, Maurianne Adams
TL51   Teaching in the Information Age: The Role of Educational Technology,
        Michael J. Albright, David L. Graf
TL50   Developing New and Junior Faculty, Mary Deane Sorcinelli, Ann E. Austin
TL49   Teaching for Diversity, Laura L. B. Border, Nancy Van Note Chism
TL48   Effective Practices for Improving Teaching, Michael Theall, Jennifer Franklin
TL47   Applying the Seven Principles for Good Practice in Undergraduate Education,
        Arthur W. Chickering, Zelda F. Gamson
TL46   Classroom Research: Early Lessons from Success, Thomas A. Angelo
TL45   College Teaching: From Theory to Practice, Robert J. Menges, Marilla D. Svinicki
TL44   Excellent Teaching in a Changing Academy: Essays in Honor of Kenneth Eble,
        Feroza Jussawalla
TL43   Student Ratings of Instruction: Issues for Improving Practice, Michael Theall,
        Jennifer Franklin
TL42   The Changing Face of College Teaching, Marilla D. Svinicki
TL41   Learning Communities: Creating Connections Among Students, Faculty,
        and Disciplines, Faith Gabelnick, Jean MacGregor, Roberta S. Matthews,
        Barbara Leigh Smith
TL40   Integrating Liberal Learning and Professional Education, Robert A. Armour,
        Barbara S. Fuhrmann

AM7/93-7L
35